D1520343

Summertime in Murdertown:
how I survived where the best die

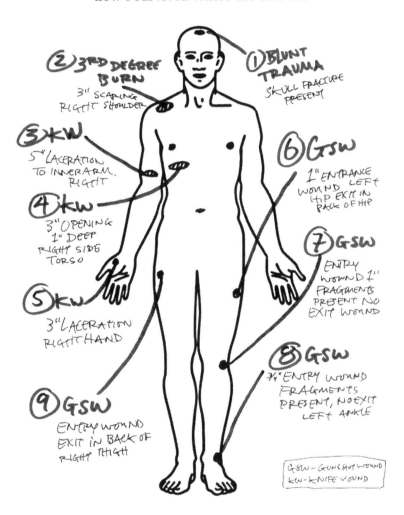

② 3RD DEGREE BURN
3" SCARING RIGHT SHOULDER

① BLUNT TRAUMA
SKULL FRACTURE PRESENT

③ KW
5" LACERATION TO INNER ARM, RIGHT

④ KW
3" OPENING 1" DEEP RIGHT SIDE TORSO

⑤ KW
3" LACERATION RIGHT HAND

⑥ GSW
1" ENTRANCE WOUND LEFT HIP EXIT IN BACK OF HIP

⑦ GSW
ENTRY WOUND 1" FRAGMENTS PRESENT NO EXIT WOUND

⑧ GSW
¾" ENTRY WOUND FRAGMENTS PRESENT, NO EXIT LEFT ANKLE

⑨ GSW
ENTRY WOUND EXIT IN BACK OF RIGHT THIGH

GSW - GUNSHOT WOUND
KW - KNIFE WOUND

a memoir by David Gunn

Summertime in Murdertown: *How I Survived Where the Best Die*
Copyright © 2019 by David Gunn

ISBN (Print): 978-1-54395-939-0
ISBN (eBook): 978-1-54395-940-6

The following is taken from several journals over the years. It isn't a biography or a complete story but snap shots from a handful of summers. Many people, insights and feelings have been left out for many reasons. I have changed the names of those in this work some out of respect some out of disrespect and some for legal reasons.

I don't want to insinuate that everyone in Flint shares my story. Thankfully that isn't the case. I only want to offer scenes and lessons from my own life and the lives of those close to me. This is how we came up... and down.

Prologue

E ight of us lived in the three bedroom house off 7th Ave in Flint's 5th ward. We didn't use many of the rooms because it was cold outside and we had no electricity. We did however have gas, so we kept the oven open to heat the house. We slept in the kitchen, all of us on two twin sized mattresses on the floor. We were seven brothers and a pregnant girl. There was a firearm for each of us in the house. An AK 47, a sawed off shotgun, 2 .357 revolvers, a .22 rifle, and 3 9mm auto handguns. Over the last few months we had signed a record deal with a major label, Roadrunner/Atlantic Records, gone on the Rockstar Mayhem Festival tour during which half of us were on the run or wanted for criminal offenses, released an album worldwide, headlined a UK European tour, and played in arenas from North America to Australia and back. We were supposed to be home gearing up for the UK Europe continuation of this tour through February 2015, visiting countries I had no clue existed. This was the furthest thing from my mind when I woke up and checked the AK 47 to make sure it was loaded. It was Christmas morning, which didn't mean anything to any of us.

1

Write About Us

I was born late December at Flint Orthopedic Hospital the same year crack cocaine was hitting the streets. That detail could've been of some significance. The hospital no longer exists which could also mean something. GM was downsizing and outsourcing and filling our rivers with toxic waste while they hurried to close their doors. I don't recall childhood all that much. A psychologist may call this repressed memory but simply knowing this doesn't conjure up new memories. I remember being passed around a lot, and moving from place to place. Grandparents, aunts and uncles, people you called aunt or uncle. I remember little details, like a peculiar house we may have stayed for a night or two. I remember taking road trips like families take and playing like children do but they usually ended in police involvement and court hearings. Needless to say, I didn't develop the deepest relationships or place the utmost trust in people very easily. I never knew when we would be packing up and moving.

This particular snapshot is from the 90's. Summertime. Summers are special in the Midwest. Most of the year is cold, wet, rainy, snowed in, so during the warm season everyone comes outside.

You could say it's when all the action happens. I lived with my mom some summers. My mom and aunt were like Thelma and Louise. I hadn't saw the film yet so I would say they more closely resembled older siblings than parental figures. Since my mom is no longer livin' that life and goes to church and all that I'll have to leave them to tell their own story. I'll do that with most people I mention. I had just arrived. It was good to be there because it was the opposite of my dad's place in the country. I had two sisters there. There were rules. You were made to go to school and come home afterward. You were told when and if you could eat and when you could drink. How long you could be outside and when to go to bed. Both parents were poor but one had structure and one was lawless in every sense of the word and then some. I thought some of the dad's and of course the step mother's punishments may have been categorized as cruel and unusual but it was just something that we had to deal with from time to time and even in the midst of being punished I cannot recall caring much. The term red headed stepchild seems appropriate here. Sometimes it was a legal custody thing where one parent had weekends and summers. Sometimes it was just an agreement that we would go here or there for a certain amount of time. We being myself and my brother Don who is a year younger. We were stuck with each other because we had the same dad, a rarity amongst over a dozen siblings. Aside from Don none of them are full blood, some are half some are step. Blood only goes so far with me. Although I have several family members I would fall on the sword for I also know and trust bums on the street better than some of my own kin so I didn't favor one over the other and still don't. Blood and strangers alike must earn love and respect. Everyone starts at zero.

I don't know how my parents met. I know they were never married but I don't recall them ever being together. I never cared to ask. My dad was that long haired guy into Metallica and Slayer and Pantera. He would expose us to all of that stuff. His wife listened to things like Acid Bath and Alanis Morissette and all that. My mom had records like Prince *Purple Rain* and R. Kelly *Twelve Play*. I learned to appreciate all of it but the music I cared most about was the stuff I would discover on my own. The music my peers turned me onto was the music of the streets. Eazy-E, 2Pac, and Biggie. The stuff that fascinated me. That spoke to us. To me, Metallica and 2Pac were the same, only 2Pac spoke right to you. Of course we could bang our heads to "Shortest Straw" and "Walk" but something moved our insides when we heard "Flint Niggaz Don't Play" by The Dayton Family. Luckily I felt the same way about music then as I do now. Why choose sides when you can have everything?

If you can't learn to respect and appreciate art of all forms you're a philistine. This became a conversation piece in our careers. The fact that hip hop and rap was ingrained in my system and would eventually make its way into my own music and have its influence, something that a "forward thinking" generation even 20 years from then could not understand or get. But more about that later. Back to the story.

When it was time to go to our mom's place we never knew where we were going or who we were going to be living with. Different house and a different boyfriend each time with a different set of siblings. For the most part though we knew we were going to Flint but sometimes ended up in Oklahoma or Florida for whatever reason. My mom was a gypsy.

I was a neighborhood kid. We had a little neighborhood crew as most kids do. My mom's boyfriend had a son, Rock, who was a lot more social than I was. He knew everyone. I was his little brother so I was immediately plugged in. One of our good friends was Face. A year or two older than us, Face was kind of a pretty boy. Not because he was stylish, we were too poor for that, but he kept his hair short instead of in a bowl cut, wore a hat and had an ear piercing. He had been beat into a folk gang a year prior and made it known to anyone and everyone. He had a little sister who was older than we were. Her name was Kara. She was cute. I had a thing for her but I kept it to myself. Kara would only fuck with gang members. One month she would be with a Crip wearing blue and the next month she would be with a Cobra wearing green. That summer it was green. I wanted in a gang. Kara was our homegirl. When the summer was over and it was time to go back to school she would suck on all our necks to give us hickeys. We thought this would appeal to the girls in school. An obvious sign that we were men instead of boys. Strange how early the social dynamic is established. Even stranger that for the most part it hasn't changed

Face and Kara lived with a family member who stayed down the road from us. Their momma, Nicole, was more of a sibling than a mother figure. She was mid-thirties, pretty, and would get thrown out of her mother's house just as much as her children. This would render them homeless, which was no big deal because us kids could always rough it on the streets or in a garage somewhere. We were used to looking after ourselves. When this happened we had no idea where Nicole would go. Sometimes she would disappear for weeks, sometimes months. She chased a bunch of men around.

I think my mom's boyfriend even messed with her but it wasn't really my business. I never made anything my business. Since I can remember I've been introverted. Stuck to myself. If there was a room full of kids I wasn't the loudest one or any kind of leader. I had no problems communicating with people but I always chose to listen rather than to speak. I liked watching. I think I always took it as an opportunity to learn something. You learn more from watching and listening than you do from speaking. Or as they say "you have two ears and one mouth for a reason."

Kara also had a friend, Kimberly, who was from the country out near my dad. She would come to town and stay for a few days but her parents were a bit more watchful. I had a crush on Kimberly too. I think everyone had a crush on everyone. As with a lot of things kids can get away with that but as an adult you're supposed to rid yourself of these natural impulses. I guess I do kind of resemble a Peter Pan. Anyway when she came to town she'd fuck with my older cousin Ugly Man who lived with us. Ugly Man was about to go to the army because he caught a case and the judge said it was either military or jail. As I write this it almost seems like a different reality. That type of shit doesn't happen anymore.

The strange coincidence about me, Face, Kara, and Kimberly is that we all bounced back and forth between the same town about 20 minutes outside of Flint. Kimberly's parents stayed there, and I have no clue who Face and Kara always ended up with but I know I would get used to seeing them. Seeing these people in my other, very different life was the only way I could stick it out in the country. It's kind of humorous to imagine a young boy compartmentalizing his various lifestyles.

Face also had a homeboy named D-Rod who was real cool and wild and down for pretty much anything. He would float around with us, sometimes every day for a week, until he would come up missing for a week or two.

The summertime routine started in the morning. If you got up early you could catch free breakfast. Like the program The Black Panthers started in the late 60's, the elementary school nearby hosted poor kids to eat "the most important meal of the day" during the summer when they were no longer in school. This was where we hung out frequently, whether at the basketball court or baseball diamond or playground. I never missed the breakfast because I was always awake first. A lot of my friends went to bed one or two hours before I got up but I would try to wake who I could. Kara was always down to go. We would ride our bikes to go and fetch our friend Dunk who lived next door to Kara's grandma. Dunk was a cool kid. He wasn't down for anything too crazy as far as breaking the law, but he was a likable cat. He was the guy on the block with the video game system. We usually played in his room when it rained

Between Dunk's house and the school was Blossom's house. Blossom's style was pure 90's like TLC in CrazySexyCool, the movie. She messed around with Rock but not exclusively. Her best friend was AJ, a tomboy who dressed like we did and played sports. Dunk had a crush on her and vice versa. AJ always rode a bike. Blossom always walked next to it.

Free breakfast was a highlight of the summer. It always kicked the day off the right way. Aside from the typical school baseball diamond, basketball court and playground, we had another place. The roof. There was some parking block poles coming out of the ground near the electrical meters. From there, we climbed up some pipes on the side of the building which led to a sublevel rooftop area. The guys had to help the girls but it was a good spot. We could see anyone coming from blocks away. On the other side between this sublevel and the primary school building was a concrete courtyard with some vegetation. This is where everyone would go to fuck or smoke cigarettes or look at the cache of porn magazines we stole from a party store around the corner. If you went in there with somebody and had a solid lookout you were set. At this point I hadn't been down there with anyone but my brother had and I was hot on his trail to make something happen. If Kara wasn't having any of my game I had my sights set on Tina who lived directly across the street from us. After going through each of the two food lines and hanging in the gym-turned-cafeteria, we would get pushed nicely outside into the parking lot and have the doors locked behind us. By 10 AM my brother was usually up.

When we needed money we would mow lawns. We always had a working lawn mower and gas. We would break engines or blades a bunch but there was a house nearby full of older cats like my brother Germ and my cousin Ugly Man. An older version of our crew, it was a house full of 18-20 year old guys and girls who were on their own. One of them was Sonny. He was what you would call a "grease monkey." Had all the tools, all the small engines, spare parts, and could fix any car. This is back when cars had parts that regular people could learn to fix by replacing a broken part with a new working part. Before they plugged cars into computers and ran some kind of program and charged you money for it.

Anyway, the older crew didn't take too kindly to us because we were "little kids" but Sonny was always nice and hooked us up. When we would get real ambitious we would try and do shit like build Frankenstein go karts and mini bikes and all that. We had a solid mower from my brother's dad but we would steal small engine machines from the pawn shop or we would break into garages and take leaf blowers and power tools and even lawn mowers. Sonny held them in his garage and worked with us on projects. Sometimes we would mow 8-10 lawns a day. We would get ten for most lawns but sometimes we would get twenty. We would only get five from the cheap old woman named Betty who lived next door. She would make you do the lawn and the leaves and the whole yard. We only did that when we were desperate. Later that year on Halloween we would put make up on like hers, which was kinda like Mimi from the Drew Carey show, and go trick or treating. When we got to her place we would knock on the door. "Trick or treat." When she asked, "What are you guys this year?" we would shout "YOU!" and take off running and laughing.

Between lawn days we would hang out and just be kids. Our side hustle was stealing bikes. If we were walking somewhere and saw a bike lying in a lawn we took it. Back at Sonny's garage, which we had come to call our shop, we would disassemble the bikes and paint them and stencil model names onto them and have signature styles and preferences. Some needed mag rims, some would don pegs to ride girls around on, and some had what we called "chrommies," just nice valve caps made of chrome or ornaments like dice or an eight ball. You would get these off semi trucks or tricked out cars a lot of the time. We never kept bikes for too long because we were always itching to sell them to get paid or to create our next new one to top the next guy. They were too easy to steal so at certain points I can remember us having a couple dozen bikes holed up in Sonny's garage, no doubt getting him bitched at by his roommates.

As an ignorant kid my money usually went one place. The girls. The Pizza and Ice Cream was the old school kind of pizza joint with the single arcade game, The Simpsons, and the picnic tables. If we weren't hanging there as a whole group I was trying to sneak off and take Tina on a "date." This just seemed like protocol with Tina, who lived across the street. She had more money than most people in the neighborhood. They had nice cars and a nice place and all that. They were solid middle class. Tina's dad hated me because I wore sweat pants and jerseys that were 2-3 sizes too big. He also knew we had to be up to no good. But her mom, who was her spitting image, liked me so I was allowed to come inside the house and all that. I would work on lawns during the day to take Tina there at night and try and get her back to the roof before it got too late. I was a risk taker too. I went lookoutless.

After a few weeks I had her on the roof, acting like I knew what I was doing. The day didn't feel like any kind of special day. Nothing extraordinary happened. After all, we had been on the roof before. But this time felt different. It was almost as if climbing up together on this particular day meant something. I think we were both trying to be cool. Trying to act like we had done this before and that it was no big deal. Trying to prove we were the more experienced and seasoned of the two of us. We kicked around small talk about our friends about what they might be doing. The sun was starting

to go down. I think it was understood that if we both kept playing around she would have to go back home. We both just went
for it.

We knew whatever it was began with kissing. That was the easy
part. I know we took each other's clothes off but things are harder
to do in tandem than they are when you're by yourself. I could pull
my own shirt off no problem but when it came to hers I messed
around and elbowed her in the face, stretching her shirt out,
caught it on her chin, pulled some ties from her hair etc. I know
I went between her legs but had no clue what to do once there. I
recall playing with condoms around this age but I didn't bother
mentioning anything of the sort much less have one on deck. I
didn't know how long this whole thing would last but I knew I
better keep slamming my mouth into hers or I would look like a
rookie. I remember our teeth hitting together over and over again
and feeling pretty reckless. I don't think I cared who saw. What
felt like the whole night probably lasted no more than 10 minutes.
When it was over I thought I was the coolest cat living. This is what
we called "fuckin." Having sex was something different, we didn't
even speak that language. Later on I told my boys in passing like it
had been happening all along but they didn't believe me because
no one was there to witness it. Still, it was only a couple days before
Tina told the neighborhood girls, including Kara so I was stamped
and certified. They all treated it like I was coming out of my shell
and joining them in the ranks. But nothing changed about me
much at all. If it came up I just brushed it off like it was something
I had been doing all along. But really I was elated. Because of this I
would find myself on the roof with Kara a week or two later, look-
out intact. This episode was much different. Kara was older and

knew a whole bunch more. I just followed her lead or more accurately I disrupted whatever rhythm she established. This episode is just as vivid but I have to save some scenes in case I decide one day to write a romance novel they can sell at CVS Pharmacy.

Naturally sex began to take up a lot of my thoughts. Word would get out to the neighborhood and my brother started taking me to hang out with Blossom and AJ, who was now dating Dunk. I remember having the urge to sleep with every girl I knew at this point. Not only that but every girl I had ever known or even ones I would just pass on the street or see in public.

I must have suddenly had some kind of game or it was just social proof that AJ let me take her to the roof one morning after breakfast. I now understood how to take control of these situations. After this it was her idea to walk over to Dunk's with me to break up with him. I just stood in the driveway. I came with his girl and left with his girl. This didn't make us any less friends to me, but on this day I learned a lesson about guys too. Some take their relationships with females a lot more serious than others. I didn't take every female encounter to heart. Having nine sisters and an out of control mom allowed me to glimpse the other side of the fence. I knew what kind of wild ride they could take you on because I had seen it firsthand. I figured they were all the same. And the cracks in what I did know were filled in by my *Eazy-Duz-It* cassette on which Eazy E reminded me often how certain types of women were to be treated. I decided a woman could make a man or destroy him if he let her.

Nothing with AJ changed things with Tina or Kara. Although it was known we were hanging out we still all went to the roof whenever we were alone. I assumed everyone was going to the roof with everyone. It made my imagination run wild at first but eventually I would grow callous to these types of things. To this day I think I take "going to the roof" more lightly than the next guy. I never took the bait of the American sex taboo.

The stuff with AJ would end when my brother got a different girl and stopped messing with Blossom. At this point I followed him to the new girl's because she had a little sister the same age as me. I might as well have been paying rent for the roof at this point.

2

Where Were You When
We Would Ride?

We would race bikes, play basketball, play video games and spray paint the school. Go to the library to check out books on odd shit. Making up songs to sing to each other. Sleep. Wake up. Do it again. We would show off for the girls by breaking glass, either bottles or windows, and running off. We would eventually get a mini bike running with a 6HP lawn mower engine and be mobile beyond our own neighborhood which wasn't always good news. And when fall came we would hide cinder blocks in the large piles of leaves on the sides of the street so dickheads who went speeding through the leaves to be cool ruined their car's front ends. Whatever we did we did it outside. We didn't hook ourselves up to a piece of technology for the majority of our days, which made our relationships much deeper.

There was plenty of other people in the crew. Mike lived down the street and was a year older and good at basketball. His older brother hung out with the older group and he had been to jail and lifted weights. There was Eric and his two sisters who lived next door to Sonny and the older cats and he was always on some interesting shit like ICP and homemade roleplaying games where you used cards and dice and all that.

Kara would soon end up with DJ. He wasn't a gang member or anything but he was older with a car. Kara was our girl which meant we now had access to a real car, not the pedal bikes and mini bikes we were piecing together. This was the first time I got behind the wheel right there in the school parking lot. DJ had taken off to walk to the party store and left the keys with his girl. She said I could hop in and drive it in a circle real quick before he got back. The party store was on the other side of the school. I hopped in excited and did what I could. I ended up smashing it into a steel guardrail. It dented it all in. Kara put the car back in place and took the blame. Anyway, DJ and Kara being together meant Heather was free game so I was over in her yard everyday trying to get her to come out and ride the mini bike with me. The whole summer would pass without taking her to the roof once.

When we had come extra money we would all try and get to the skate rink, asking my mom's boyfriend to drive or all pile into DJ's car. We were all good at skating and it was fun when they played shit like Coolio's "Gangstas Paradise" or Dr. Dre's "Keep They Heads Ringing." Sometimes the skating rink even had "lock ins" where they got a couple sets of bleachers and locked everyone in until morning. We would eat popcorn and hotdogs and drink sodas all night while trying to get girls under the bleachers. I always stood guard for Aaron and if I wasn't doing that I was guarding for a neighborhood kid named Shannon who was alright. One day we had a falling out, though, because someone told him about me being under the bleachers with his younger sister. She hypnotized me. I had watched her skate in circles for weeks, illuminated by all the colors from the par can lighting, lip syncing "Wonderwall" by Oasis. This was irresistible. It was confusing how he couldn't understand that every female was somebody's sister.

We would go to the skate rink with an old pair of shoes, a pair that had been your brother's in the garage or taken off someone's porch on your way to skate. You gave the skate rental your shoes and a dollar or two for a pair of rental skates. Now the doors could only be opened from outside the building. Near the end of the night we would have a mark all scoped out, usually one mark each. Everyone had a target. Some soft ass middle aged white man with his kids or some couple we didn't know. When our ride home was a friend he would walk into the building and tie his shoes in the doorway. This gave us a 15-20 second window. We would skate as fast as we could toward the mark with the beeper and ultimately toward the door. Flying by the mark we would snatch the beeper from his hip. Guys with beepers in these days wore them facing outward big and bulky like they do with the big smartphone cases now. Street smart individuals would always wear them clip out with the beeper on the inside. We snatched these things almost instantaneously and all fly out the door with a new pair of roller-blades and a new beeper. Some of us were so smooth they didn't notice their beeper was missing until we caused a scene flying out the entrance door. No cameras, no ID's, nothing like that. Doing this move meant we had to stay away from the skating rink for a few months or until we would get word that they hired a new staff of high schoolers.

In the coming year this would land me the green skyway pager. I immediately put the 2Pac sticker on it. You used to be able to make collect calls from pay phones to pagers free of charge. We had codes to put in, 911 for emergency, 211 for some kind of money making opportunity to meet up in the garage or 000 to meet at the Pizza and Ice Cream.

When we weren't getting into trouble we would do things like spend the night in a tent in the backyard. Me and my siblings and our friends. It was our mom's boyfriend's job to watch us, which he didn't take too seriously and we all loved him for it. He was more of a friend than an authority figure which meant we would listen to MC Breed and Top Authority while playing stupid games like suck and blow with a library card. A few of us would try and stay up as late as possible to mess around with the girls. When Tina was around she got my attention over the next girl. Word that I messed around with her in the tent would eventually get around to her parents, which got her grounded. This would teach me that messing around with girls works when you're alone or with a close homeboy. Letting others into your business is detrimental. I decided secrets were kinda like women. Some you'd share and they'd get passed around but others would go to the grave with you if necessary.

I was at Heather's as usual, trying to get her to kick it with me. At this point I could get her onto her porch but that wasn't good enough. On my way home I saw the boys at the pizza joint. DJ was there. He and Face had a plan. They wanted to break into a house. In two weeks. And they needed as many people as they could get. It was me, Face, DJ, and D-Rod. I don't remember if my brother thought this was a stupid idea or not. He was usually down for whatever bullshit we might get into. He wasn't present and I didn't want to do anything without him but I knew I wanted to go on this exciting stuff, simply because it was exciting and I was curious. In hindsight I think they only included me because of the strides I was making with girls. The strange thing about having so many sides to you is the people who have one side in common mistake your parts for a whole and pin you as whatever is comfortable for them. I didn't seek the approval of the bad kids and freeze out the good ones. I was friends with everyone but I was down for anything.

We would end up taking our planning session to the garage because the Pizza and Ice Cream parking lot was filling up outside. Dunk was there with AJ. They had started hanging out again which was probably for the better. I had been messing with Blossom since my brother got the new girlfriend so my confidence was through the ceiling. Anyway, the word was there were several guns in this house. I didn't know how DJ got this information but I had no choice but to believe it. Me, Face, and D-Rod would go inside and DJ would be the getaway driver. When we got away clean we would each have our choice of which gun we wanted and DJ could sell the rest to the older cats. This would go down in two weeks. I was given one instruction between now and then and that was to find out if the place had a dog or not. A dog would be a big deterrence. So that week I was supposed to grab my lawn mower and go knocking on the door. If I didn't hear one barking from the inside to try and look past whoever answered. If I could mow the lawn I should mow the lawn and look for any signs of a dog, like a dog house in the yard or a chain or something. I was also told to look-out for extra shit we might be keen on taking.

Over the next week I walked by every day to get the balls to do the recon. I had reservations about it and came up with another excuse each passing day. One day I thought I saw a car there. Another day I didn't see anyone home. Each day I was grilled by the team on whether or not I was capable of handling the task. They were growing impatient but at the same time they weren't running to take my place. Maybe it was a test or maybe it was some older kids just using me for the shitty part of the job. There wasn't a question if I was going to do it or not I think I just knew I had time and was apprehensive. Eventually I went up to the door and knocked and waited. Nervous. No one answered. I walked away, planning to come back later and try again like I had so many times before. I would do this once more in the next week and get the same result. Even when I saw a car in the driveway, no answer. I snooped around from the sidewalk looking for clues. Nothing. This was as much investigation as I thought I could conduct. The day was getting too close and I had wasted too much time. I would tell my friends there was no dog and it was safe. I remember them grilling me on what the man was like and I just used every bit of common sense I had and said an old man. I guess I thought a young man like us or like DJ wouldn't have his own house and a nice car with several guns in it.

Two weeks felt like a lifetime after that. We talked about our plan every day. Almost like our interpretation of something from Mission Impossible, the first one. I couldn't really focus on much else aside from this. Ugly Man worked at the donut shop while waiting to ship out. He would bring home big boxes of donuts after work early in the morning. I think it was his way of contributing to the household because he lived in the basement and always had Kimberly over but didn't pay no rent or bills, so that was his offering. I would normally eat 5-6 of them but I remember not even feeling it around this time. I remember not trying to take any girls to the roof either. I was fully focused in on the whole idea. I couldn't get the mission off my mind and it kept me from loosening up and being a kid. I didn't know it then but this "job" would be a transitional act for us.

We pulled down the street and DJ turned the car off. We must've seen every cop in Flint on the drive there. We talked about how they must be onto us. How did they know. And it sure seemed like there were many more than usual out patrolling the streets. I remember being nervous as each of us took a side of the house we didn't think was a bedroom. We started messing with the windows all around the house trying to get a way in. Mine was locked tight so I went to the next one on the same side of the house. I spent what seemed like minutes looking around before messing with the window for ten seconds. I was shit out of luck so I started circling the house. I wanted to go back to the car but when I turned a corner I noticed the boys had a window open and were proceeding to climb through. We slid through with no problem, as you do when you're a kid. Once inside I stood still, not breathing, taking everything in, trying to make sense of the layout which looked like a foreign space station for what seemed like minutes before snapping out of this hypnotism. There were no dog barks so I was relieved. The house smelled kind of like old people so I was in luck there too. Only thing I could think to do was follow Face. I didn't know what I was doing. I was in a house I had never been in. Didn't know where to go, who was inside and if they were awake or not or if they knew we were in their house or not. In hindsight we should've just waited until no one was home to do this. That is the difference between "breaking and entering" and "home invasion," which is a much more serious crime but kids are kids.

I followed Face into a room with no door on it. It had a wood and glass gun case in it with the key and chain in the lock. The lock was a formality that didn't really secure the case anymore than the thin wood or the glass of the armoire. This is why the primitive key sat in the lock. Either that or someone had just visited the case. I stared on as Face opened it and started handing me hunting shotguns and rifles, four total, but Face handed me three and carried one. The first time you're always nervous about getting caught. That comes with the disadvantages you have and your imagination playing into it. Not knowing the floor plan, not knowing where the exits are, not knowing who we were dealing with. You have the feeling once you're in and it immediately goes away when you're outside and free, but we were far from free. I can't remember how long ago I had this thought but it's strange how people flee when they're seen doing something wrong. For example there were a few of us. If the old man appeared we could probably take him and continue on and better our chances of a clean getaway rather than running and giving the authorities a chance to get involved but I know we all would've taken off if we heard so much as an unusual voice. It could be the guilt you have when doing something you're not supposed to be doing that causes the able bodied man to run from the elderly woman when she's spotted stealing or a kid running from a smaller kid when caught stealing a bike from him. I don't know if it's the guilt of the act or the unwillingness to take the act further. Anyway we hadn't alerted anyone to my knowledge though the guns I carried clanked together while Face collected things in the living room. A VCR. Yeah, I'm serious. D-Rod was nowhere to be found, but we had tunnel vision so he could've been standing next to me the whole time for all I knew. I recall not being as smooth as I anticipated and making more noise than I wanted to. You gain control over your senses in these situations with frequency.

Face got something which we guessed to be gold or jewelry from the kitchen counter and our hands were full. We made our way over to the window and crawled out one at a time with our hands full of shit. No D-Rod in sight. We were outside and there was no way we were going back in. We ran to the car and threw the shit in the backseat and got in. We argued about who should go back and check on D-Rod. They always used the same excuse on me. You're the youngest, if you get caught you can't get charged, they can't charge kids your age with crimes and if they do, they fall off your record at 18 and you get a fresh start. I believed this shit so I hopped out of the car. Once outside the car I heard noise and yelling so I ran. I jumped in the car and we all heard one single gunshot. DJ fired up the car and floored it. I stared out the window as we pulled away and didn't see anything. We screamed and yelled and argued the mile back to Face's grandma's house where the next door neighbor had a broke down boat in the driveway. This was the boat that had been there 15 years and the only water it probably saw in our lifetime was the pitiful washes of rain on it. This is where we hid the guns, under the tarp. I told Face I'd sneak him into the basement and we would sleep there. I don't know if we actually slept that night but I remember sitting up for a while and replaying the whole thing in my head. Talking it over and over again. Playing out scenarios that D-Rod may be in. Did he get caught. Did he get shot. I imagined his dead body and his funeral. How I would feel were he dead and how I would react etc. It was a turning point in life I didn't understand at the time. Nowadays more poetically I would describe it as some kind of loss of innocence. Of course before this we were having sex or what we thought was sex, but I don't think mental and physical children acting out sex with other children without a certain understanding constitutes a loss of innocence. Also we were stealing pagers and bicycles and things like that, and although we thought we were real gangsters, this felt like something much heavier. We had crossed a line. This was the big leagues. Hearing that shot and not knowing if it was fired into my friend's body changed my thinking. This shit was for keeps. I wanted more. I wanted to take it to the extreme as with anything I did. Since most of the kids were older I was in a hurry to grow up. Now I'm anything but.

The next morning I got a page. The code was 23. Stood for Michael Jordan, the goat. It meant get to the school basketball court. I woke Face up. He usually wouldn't have been out this early but today he listened to me. D-Rod was at the court. I was more than relieved.

He was excited and telling his crazy story over and over again. Something to the tune of seeing a handgun in the bedroom on some kind of table or nightstand. I didn't look into this room at all so I have no idea, but he said he ran in and grabbed it and they woke shocked and he took off running. He said he flew toward the back door and the man gave chase. Before he could get the door unlocked, he shot the revolver in the house on accident, through the floor. The old man stopped in his tracks and he got away on foot but was pissed and blaming us for leaving him. Finally, he admitted to running in the complete opposite direction and didn't even check for the car. At first I was in disbelief but D-Rod had the revolver in DJ's car with all the rest of the guns. Apparently DJ went and collected the whole score and was driving around with it. If I were sharper at the time I would've seen this as a red flag but it made me instantly proud to have helped and been a part of the job. I didn't fuck anything up. We had five guns total. One a piece. Of course I got the worst pick, a hunting rifle, but I was more than happy with it at the time.

Later that night the whole crew was in the garage just telling the story over and over again from different perspectives jumping all over the soiled couch while glamorizing their role in the heist and showing off the guns. The next idea was to saw them off like we had heard of people doing to conceal them better in our pants. The dynamic kind of changed that night. Everyone looked at us differently, even amongst our group and I could feel it although others didn't seem to notice. There was a line drawn in the sand and some of the crew weren't feeling our heist. Some thought it was stupid. Some worried for one reason or another. Some completely embraced it. I was indifferent to the way people felt because it didn't change anything about us or about our relationships. About the crew. Anyway, the heist did have some positive effect. Heather seemed drawn to me suddenly. Her mom was never home so we went right to her room. I remember Kara was still down too. Kara never stopped being down. I took it the same way I took everything, in stride. I wouldn't go play video games at Dunk's as much as I used to. Tina wasn't as keen on me as before either. After a month or so I remember everyone kind of shifting back to normal. We were the same kids again. But as with everything I continued to take notes on people and the way they behaved.

We lost one gun quick. No one knows how but it just came up missing. This was just before a cousin was involved in a neighborhood party store robbery that ended fatally. The store was the target of a lot of snatch and runs therefore they had recently taken up arms in an attempt to deter thieves from running off with their merchandise. After the clerk reached for his gun the robber panicked and shot the clerk dead and ran. He would eventually be caught and sent off to prison. We didn't know if there was a correlation so we just kept it to ourselves.

We rolled around now with all the guns on us and in the car. We were ready for anything. I can't remember how long it took but we soon found out that shit was going to hit the fan. The house we had robbed had been some kind of cop or retired cop. Our names were hot and everyone knew who did it. By DJ's reaction I would still to this day guess he had no clue this was a cop's house, no one knew. I didn't even question how this news got out there but we couldn't afford to brush it off. We had four pieces of gun barrels we had to get rid of. We also had to hide the guns back in the boat. In the coming week or so the rumors had developed into the old man having some kind of sound recording equipment in his house. We were doomed. I don't know why we all believed this.

All the older cats really took a liking to us and tried to get the guns off us. Namely my cousin and his friends. They were tired of doing stick ups with fake guns. They had recently pulled a fake gun on a Crip and been shot at over it. We weren't having it though their old asses could fend for themselves. We never took them in the house or let them around our cache. During this time D-Rod and DJ were taking shit to the next level doing stickups on people outside the bars on the main road. They would get wallets and purses and cash then move on to the next place. That wasn't my bag and I can't remember Face ever doing it either. We didn't aim to hurt any regular people. Just the people we had problems with. For whatever reason that may be. At that age I didn't have a wisdom behind it but now I know better than to bring squares into this kind of lifestyle. Having square allies is fine but giving them access to any illicit information or putting them into a compromising situation is putting a burden on them they may not be able to handle once pressure is applied. This puts you in jeopardy. The person who shares incriminating information or secrets or gossip with others may be viewed as a friend by those he's sharing it with but in reality he is sprinkling burdens on everyone he speaks to. Having a square as a victim who doesn't live by the same rules and codes well, the law is usually their go to. This also puts you in jeopardy. I decided I should try to avoid integrating outsiders whether as victims or allies into the street ecosystem.

I didn't carry the sawed off everywhere I went. After a few weeks it wore off and I still wanted to play basketball and do the lawns and hang out with girls. Not keep digging in my pants trying to readjust my set up every minute or two. During this time my older brother would carry it. I wouldn't think about it until shit would really pop off.

The gang scene was in full effect as a kid. A lot of Bloods on the Southside. Boys in red who appeared to be predominantly black. The east had the East Side Crips with the blue and the Cobras were in green. They were both predominantly Hispanic but both contained some black dudes and some white boys. The north side was and still is more about the neighborhoods. The 5th ward, Pierson Hood, Civic Hood, Merrill Hood, Selby Hood and so on which were mostly black. I had respect for everyone from any hood in Flint but knew the most Crips and north end boys.

One day we were playing basketball with kids we didn't know. My little brother got scored on so he spit on a kid. The kid noticed and tripped out. My older brother stepped in and convinced the kid he didn't do it and the game went on. When the game was over the younger group of kids started to leave, screaming shit when they were a distance away. They started throwing gang signs. Face and everyone threw opposing signs back. The group kept walking. When it was dusk our friends would leave. I never wanted to leave. I stayed on the playground as late as anyone would hang with me. I heard 2Pac from DJ's car moving off in the distance. The ones that did stay with me and Face and the girls were driving off to the party store around the corner.

This was the worst time for us to be away from the car where the guns were stashed. The kid my brother spit on went home to his older brother who was a member of a Blood gang and told him what happened. He was pissed. Now there was a gray Camaro circling the schoolyard. We knew something was up when it turned and started driving through the playground toward us. It stopped quick about twenty yards from us. Everyone inside wore red and we knew one of them. I was with a known gang member so I was running right along with him. Face flicked his Nike sandals off and we ran through the neighborhood leaving the girls in the dust. These guys were older than both of us and faster. We were going toward my place. I never stopped to count how many there were.

I was focused on running. But I must have looked back because I was blowing through someone's front yard and I tripped on those little steel pieces of ankle-high lawn ornaments people line their sidewalks with. I busted my face on the ground and thought I was hit. I felt someone grab me from the back, hold me up and say "What?! BK?!" A reference to a "blood killa" sign Face threw prior. He dropped me and started chasing Face along with his homeboys. Face got away. Not me. I would get my ass whooped. I got punched a few times and just balled up while they kicked me for a minute before realizing they were in some woman's front yard and took off.

This wouldn't bother me at all. I remember being excited and proud that I had just been jumped by an older gang. Up to this point I had only gotten into playground fights in elementary school. I remember feeling official. I knew I wasn't a gang member but I had taken a beating for a gang member friend and it felt good, minus the petty wounds. Fighting would become something I was drawn to after this. Revenge would be another.

When DJ and the boys rode back to the basketball court the girls told them what happened. They pulled up to our place about the same time I got back home. My mom's boyfriend covered for me while I cleaned myself up. We knew we had to retaliate but we didn't know exactly how it was done. Someone suggested we go right back up to the school and see if they were still in the area. We would be standing our ground. I was down with any kind of proactive plan. I wanted to stand tall and prove to everyone around me that I could be counted on even when shit hit the fan. Shit felt exciting. I recalled the way our more cautious friends acted after we robbed the house. It changed the dynamic. I wasn't going to be the reason shit fell apart. I considered the crew all I had. Whatever these guys got into I was going to go head first into and probably go the hardest. I don't think I understood it at the time. Obviously I didn't comprehend social dynamics, Freudian concepts or conduct disorders. I couldn't put any of this into words but I recall vividly thinking there was no way I wasn't standing tall next to these guys.

We went back up there deep, this time with the guns, hoping they would come back. It was starting to get darker but we could hear a car playing loud music in the distance. The school took up half a city block so you could see three or four different streets around its border. Across the field someone made out the gray Camaro. At this time we're on the basketball court with the car parked on center court. D-Rod and Face start throwing up six pointed stars and folks up signs at the car. I see someone hanging out of the window twisting their fingers up from the passenger of the two door as it turned a corner and headed closer toward us. I say fuck it and go to the car to get a gun. Sawed shotgun. Hunting style. Not a pump. I kept it hanging by my leg. I didn't know how to shoot, never shot before, didn't know about accuracy and range and other factors. At this point I only knew that my nerves were flying as I stood underneath the hoop with the gun in hand. They started walking across the field maybe fifty yards off. At this point I knew there were five of them. DJ said fuck this and hopped in his car and took off. I had no clue why but the rest of us stayed there, armed. When they got close enough, I noticed the one in the front had a handgun in his hand hanging by his side. He was the smallest of the group and the loudest. We could hear him at this point. They must have realized they were out gunned. Whether anyone would shoot was beside the point. The group stopped in their tracks and stood for a minute. A few of them threw up more gang signs and talked more shit. Then they turned and started walking away, looking over their shoulder at us from across the way. We were gassed up and on edge. We checked them but we still didn't prove a point. D-Rod took a few steps toward them with his gun. This made them all turn around and face us. I saw D-Rod raise his gun so I raised mine, immediately pointed toward the group. I closed my eyes and squeezed. The gun jumped. I was holding it as tight as I could and I still didn't control it. When I opened my eyes the group was running. They hadn't shot back. I don't think they even thought about it. They took off.

I stood there disoriented as my friends ran around me. I don't recall how many shots were fired. I ran along with the rest of them toward the neighborhood. I remember throwing the gun instinctively. We made it back to the garage. All of us. This was just as exciting and crazy as the robbery job that we were jumping all over excited about retelling it from all angles. We thought we were something. It felt good to me that I could be counted on. At the time it was the most serious thing that had happened to me. We didn't hit any of them, this I knew. They were all running and I had guessed you kind of feel when a bullet you shoot connects into something. Like any hunter knows. In hindsight we had no aim no skills and we were shooting at kids at least thirty yards or more away. None of this was the point. From here on out we considered ourselves grown. I don't mean to romanticize crime to inspire others but I personally had fallen in love with it. It's a real life game with real life stakes and it has no rules. Some people try to say the streets have rules but they just mean they themselves have rules. In reality the streets have no rules because some people in them have none so you have to play to that level or you lose. Crime has such a charm as a youth. It's more attractive than any woman and more desirable than any material possession.

We would lose a second gun thereafter. This girl Wanita would con us out of it. My brother wanted to date her and she was always trying to buy my shotgun. She was way out of our usual league, much older, seventeen, and developed and all that. Big bro wanted me to sell it to her because he thought it would better his chances, so I did. He took her to the roof. This was a hood rat though so of course there was a problem. She was fucking with him and wanted the gun so she could give it to the blood who just whooped my ass. Now they were just as armed as our group.

Within a couple days we would see the kid we spit on at a party. The gang member's little brother. None of his brothers were around so we attacked him. I had a newfound appreciation for fighting so I did my best amongst the group to inflict damage. Being highly competitive I always had to take shit one step further. When the kid was down I picked up a broom that was laying nearby. I pointed the handle at his stomach and slammed down the tip of the handle like one would when digging a hole with a shovel. This was my second real fight and I was starting to get the hang of it.

Once I crossed the threshold of illicit activities it was easy to start letting them snowball one after another. The last memory I have from this summer was an altercation that would lead to my first arrest. I was riding my bike around the neighborhood. A group of kids down the street called me over. I knew it was probably a bad idea but I didn't care. I was feeling myself. As I got closer I recognized them from my old school. I hopped off and we exchanged words about the bike. One of the kids pulled out a pellet gun. One of the rifles you pump to increase the power and shoot little pellets. He put it to my bike tire and asked what I would do if he shot my tire out. I encouraged him to try it and find out. Since I was outnumbered he probably figured he had good odds. He shot the pellet and my tire flattened immediately. I calmly turned away and walked my bike the five or six blocks back to my aunt's house while they shouted and laughed behind me. I went to get my brother. He was at his mom's house on the other side of the neighborhood with one of his friends. He knew the kids himself and we came up with a simple plan. DJ and the real guns had since came up missing and we had to do something now. These were some punk kids with BB guns anyway so my brother and his friend suggested we come back with the same. He had a co2 powered pellet gun. It was a pistol style. You put a co2 cartridge in the handle and it could shoot semi-automatic without pumping it.

We stuffed the handgun in our pants and walked across the neighborhood once again feeling ourselves. On the walk that ol' familiar rush returned. Someone was about to get fucked up. We went back to the corner but they were nowhere to be found. We walked further down the street to a dead end that was headed off by a gravel trail. The trail went under a train track and led to a woodsy area. We saw them playing on the tracks. It was even better than we had planned. We hopped off into the woods and headed toward the group. When we got close enough we watched and waited for a good opportunity. Bro had the pellet gun. We looked at each other and hopped out of the bushes. He raised the gun up and I yelled some stupid shit to blow our cover and cause hysteria. He started shooting in their direction and they were completely caught off guard. They dropped their gun and fell to the ground. As we slowly walked toward them he kept shooting and I kept yelling at them. One took off running and the rest were frozen on the ground awaiting our instructions and yelling because they had been hit. My brother's boy took the gas pistol and told them to stand up and walk towards the woods. They listened and we followed. I don't think either of us knew the plan at that point. I was bugging him. I kept asking him for the gun. I was still pissed and in my mind hadn't got any revenge. They ignored me.

There was ample junk in the woods. It was a teenage hang out. The homeboy spotted a bathtub and told them to get into it. They tried but couldn't fit and started begging for us to let them go. One of the kids was crying. I knew him from school and he was going with a friend of mine. He always dissed me to this girlfriend of his and I wished she could have been there to see her boyfriend crying like a little girl. After a few minutes we realized the one that got away would surely be back with some older kids in their crew. I was still asking for the pellet gun over and over again and they finally gave in. I pointed it at the group of kids still pissed and started shooting. I don't know how many times. The kids were jumping all over and screaming and running. Finally we ran back towards the house, trying to keep the gun from falling out of our pants. We made it home safely. Since we thought we were in the clear we went to our backyard and filled some Sprite 2 liters with water to use as targets and discussed the recent happenings. It wasn't but 10 or 15 minutes before the police rolled in with their guns drawn yelling for us to get down. We were taken to the police station and questioned over and over. They separated us and threatened to charge us with kidnapping and assault with a deadly weapon and this and that. Eventually we would be released, probably because of our age. My brother said I never carried the pellet gun and took the heat for it. My mom and her boyfriend picked us up from the police station. To this day they haven't mentioned the incident.

The summer was coming to an end. Soon I would be relocated back to my dad's for the school year. In the country and away from all the action. My parents didn't share much with each other at all. I lived a double life. I spent every day in the country writing rap songs about my 3 incidents and counting down to the next time I would return to Flint. I wanted nothing to do with living in the middle of nowhere. I felt like I was born to be running the streets with the crew. To be living fast. I felt like I had found a purpose. Living with my dad was like a jail sentence that I had to wait out until the next time I could return.

When I did come back things were much different. My mom and her boyfriend would separate and I would lose touch with my brother and most other people as well.

Over the years I would learn that Face and Kara would be sent to the country. Face would end up in jail. Kara with a few kids.

Ugly Man would disappear, either to the military or on the run. I haven't seen him since.

Kimberly would be sent back home and become a dancer when she was old enough. I haven't seen her since.

D-Rod would go to jail soon after. I haven't seen him since.

DJ would kill a kid a couple years down the line and go to prison. I haven't seen him since.

Dunk moved out of state and faired alright.

AJ would move away.

Blossom would get hooked on drugs.

The older cat who whooped my ass, who now had the shotgun, would saw it off shorter. He was testing shooting it in his back yard to make sure it was functional. When he backed the gray Camaro out of the driveway the cops were waiting for him to take him away.

That summer I was 10 years old.

3

Sing Me To Sleep

Not much time would pass before I would stop bouncing back and forth and settle myself in for good. After a couple uneventful years I got caught stealing from the school. During lunch, my friends and I would separate and sit at opposing sides of the gym. From there we could all get away with asking to use the bathroom at the same time. This would allow us to go into the hall and make a break for our nearby classroom. Once inside we would go through the teacher's desk and cabinets. Sometimes we would get lucky and score an envelope of book club money.

One day we stumbled upon something aside from the usual pens and markers and seven loose dollars. We opened the desk drawer to find a Polaroid laying right on top of everything. The photograph was of our teacher. Naked. We sat there staring at it not knowing what to do. One of my friends picked it up and stuffed it into his pocket and we took off out of the room to get back to lunch. I think he still has it today. Maybe she left it there for us. That wasn't the last straw at school though. The last heist went as follows.

Our classroom had an iguana as a class pet. At the end of the day a kid would go and get iguana food from the teacher's lounge down the hall. The kid usually elected to get the food was sick, so I volunteered. I don't know why the teacher allowed this, after all this was the naked teacher, but she did. I walked down the hall and into the lounge. Once inside I was by myself. The refrigerator was off in the corner but I was stopped in my tracks by the opportunities that surrounded me. Candy bars, chips, sodas. I couldn't pass it up. I filled every pocket I had with a dozen or so candy bars. Not wanting to take too long I retrieved the food from the refrigerator and returned to class with it. I came back to school the next day with a plan.

At the end of the day I volunteered to get the food again. This time I wore my jacket in there and once inside I filled every pocket I had available. Once they were full I walked calmly across the hall to the bathroom. I hopped on top of the urinal and stuffed every last candy bar up into the drop ceiling and returned to do it again. I damn near cleaned the whole place out before returning to the class with the food. The next day before the first class I stopped in the bathroom to load up my backpack with about 60 candy bars. In the morning the kids just hang out in the halls waiting for their teachers to come unlock the classroom and let everyone in. I hit the halls selling candy bars for a dollar. I sold out. I went back to the bathroom to restock and continued selling before the teacher came to let us in class. The crowd around me in the halls or the fact that everyone had a candy bar on them must have been a red flag. The teacher went through my backpack while I was in gym class that day and I was called to the office. I would have to be suspended. They must have thought I was giving the shit away because they didn't ask for or look for any money that I had. I was bummed out because since I believed the naked photo was left for us I believed I could potentially hook up with the teacher which was a goal I had for many obvious reasons. After that, my dad dropped me and Don on my mom's front lawn. Or what he thought was her front lawn. He didn't know where she was living at the time because they didn't talk to each other at all. We didn't know where she lived exactly because we couldn't track her down. Most of the times when she was due for her weekend she never showed and kept us waiting on the steps. After a few hours of sitting on the lawn we started walking around the neighborhood with our bags like a couple bums. When we got hungry we went to the corner 7-Eleven to get some food with my small fortune. And there was my mom. She was briefly surprised but we hopped in the car and she took us home bitching about our dad. I was back in the fold.

We moved often, sometimes six or eight times a year. New boyfriend, new brothers and sister, new neighborhood. Several of my old friends were in jail at this point. It's just part of the culture I guess. If it wasn't jail, we were separated by something else, death. It was around this age that people I knew were getting killed or killing themselves either on purpose or with drugs. It soon became part of who we were. Not even my grandma would die of old age. She was run down by a car. One day you'd have a friend in the neighborhood and the next day they would be on a missing persons poster around town. At the time of this writing and with my skill I don't feel I can accurately depict the pain of then and now. I attempt to do so in music which works to some degree but writing about pain in its scope would be like attempting to write about

God. It becomes overwhelming immediately. Pain as a human constant is unavoidable. Deal with it. As I grew older I started living in my head more, as people do. I started formulating my own philosophies.

We lived on the Northwest side of town, where I felt most comfortable. This is where I was born and felt at home no matter how much I moved around. My aunt lived next door to us. She watched over us. Mostly we were free to do whatever we wanted with our days. At this age we spent most of our time trying to sneak into girls' houses. If our mom did happen to be home we would try and steal the car and joy ride around the city. Our house was full of siblings and friends.

When I wasn't at home I was staying at Yon's house a couple miles down Clio Road. Yon lived with his dad whom I considered my dad. He had a girlfriend and a few other kids who I considered siblings. He wasn't home much because he was busy in a motorcycle gang and I assume always getting into some shit of his own. I wished he was my dad because he was a gangster. His ol lady didn't tell him what to do. He didn't sit around the house playing video games. He was in control of shit.

Back in Flint, we immediately started raising hell and causing problems for everyone. I recall Child Protective Services chasing us around town to every house and every school we attended. Any poor kid knows CPS is the enemy. If they were let into the house it was over. How old are all of you? Are you here alone? Where are your parents? How come there's no food in the house? How many of you sleep in this room? How come you aren't in school?

We all knew foster care would be the next step. Now I understand they were just doing their jobs but when they showed up on the doorstep we knew to cut all the lights out and stay away from the windows while they knocked for as long as they could tolerate. When they rolled up on us in the street we knew either not to talk to them or to run in any direction but home. They were as bad as the cops.

Around late spring time one of my closest friends, MDS, who was just a little older than me, had a job washing dishes at Angelo's Coney Island on Davison and Franklin. He would hook me up washing dishes and teaching me how to cook when there was nothing else to do. Between the two of us we would work every day from 10 AM to 8 PM. As far as child labor laws were concerned kids our age weren't even supposed to work, let alone 40-50 hours a week, but this was before all the social movements like truancy or bullying or children suing their parents for hitting them to name a few. Not to be insensitive toward these topics but when I discovered that Abraham Lincoln had quit school at 12 I would make every effort to quit at that age, initially quitting in 6th grade. It wouldn't go very smooth I would end up having to do a couple more years before dropping out for good in the 9th grade. On top of that I believed bullying had created droves of extraordinary people. Without these kinds of dynamics, we get what we have today, which is a slightly more animated version of George Orwell's *1984*. Anyway, there was plenty of violence going on but no one sued anyone where I lived and hardships forged unique individuals and things went on as so. We showed up to work and were paid cash and for some young boys 200 dollars a week was a good payday. The job was on the east side. We lived on the north.

This would mean that if I were working there everyday I would have to make the move to the east and move in with MDS near the coney island within walking distance because my mom sure as hell wasn't around to give me a ride every morning across town.

MDS lived no different than we did. Single mom with kids. His house had no electricity so we lit candles inside at night. We kept a cooler in the kitchen and ate things like cans of corn for dinner which didn't bother me at all. The night before my first day when we laid down to sleep, MDS explained to me that at work we could eat whatever we wanted. They took a dollar a day out of your "check" for food and on top of that a lot of customers didn't finish their plates so we could bus the table and keep any leftovers for ourselves.

On the first day I walked in, I got a couple t-shirts with the company name on them and started washing dishes. There was no interview or screening process or orientation. Our schedule was written in pencil on the wall. Our time cards were in the kitchen under the time clock. The guys that worked there were anywhere from my age to 50. We would work alongside a wide array of characters. Some cooks fighting murder charges, some deadbeat dads dodging child support payments by working an under the table job, some retired men who would do anything to get away from their wives and kids, some illegal immigrants, some just regular people. Anyway, it wasn't a hard job. We just stood there spraying dishes reciting our favorite songs, you know, dumb shit. The highlight of the day was when they would ask me to run to the warehouse to get supplies. This was more like a residential house neighboring the restaurant. Inside it had steel shelves and I would have to retrieve stuff like mustard and grease. Sometimes I would find a tub of syrup spilled over and live mice or rats stuck in it by their hair kicking and squirming around. This was about as exciting as work got.

After work our main activity was listening to music. Our CD player was in a broken down car. It just sat in the driveway and didn't ever move. It did, however, have a working battery and we sat in there listening to music, sometimes turning the volume down to holler back and forth at a homeless man named "Chill." He was always "chillin." Sometimes on a porch, sometimes in a lawn, sometimes he would even be up in a tree. I don't recall seeing him in motion moving from these places which is maybe where he got his name. The conversation went something to the tune of "What's up, Chill?" "Chillin" he would say. "Hell yeah." Then we would turn the music back up. Undoubtedly a rap CD we bought with our work pay, *The Marshall Mathers LP*, or one I picked up from around the house.

We really explored music in that broke down car in the driveway. We had the same pop sensibility all kids have I guess. There was no stigma about genre. I would take CD's laying around my mom's place. I played *Purple Rain* until there were little burn marks in the disc. That CD made me feel happy for some reason. I was curious about artists from Michigan. Aretha Franklin, Stevie Wonder, Madonna, Bob Seger, Alice Cooper and Marvin Gaye, who was Motown so we'll take him all the same, were trance-inducing. The Temptations were enchanting. I felt like I had missed out for so many years and it was time to catch up.

Yon showed me the White Stripes from Detroit. I thought what Jack and Meg were doing was genius. Artists like Outkast blew my mind. They were rapping, but you could hear the band, the drums and the horns underneath. On top of this their melodies were weird and sometimes felt off key yet Andre was so natural that no one batted an eye. The music was a hybrid and its very own thing all at once. We liked the songs we felt. I remember it was exciting to catch Eminem's "The Way I Am" video on TV and see Marilyn Manson and Eminem on the same screen mixing their worlds together. Rock music had a lane and would appear on television shows like TRL right alongside Britney Spears and N'Sync. Korn and RAGE seemed like the biggest bands in the world to us. Nine Inch Nails was my favorite. They were rock stars, almost of a different world. We would be engulfed in this stuff and it would damn near have us floating away. But we never got too out of touch with what was right in front of us. The Dayton Family *What's on my Mind* was a cassette that talked about the very streets we knew. C-Murder *Life or Death* talked about the things people around us were a part of. Back in these days you would walk into a CD store and buy an album based on what it looked like, believe it or not. There was no downloading. There was no listening station in the store. I remember buying the Bloods & Crips *Bangin' on Wax* CD we found in a store called Harmony House because the people on the cover looked like the people I had come up around. As appealing and over the top and artistic as Slipknot was there was always an Esham cassette to pull the string on the balloon back down to reality. Thus the ingredients mixed.

Music felt progressive. There was innovation around every corner. Perhaps it was because I was young but I felt like artists were pushing ahead into uncharted territory. Whether it was heavy rock, hip hop, rap, pop whatever new things were churning and developing. I learned that art is not about comfort. The foundation of any art form is hard work which is why I would say today what is called "innovative" is just new in age and different not necessarily innovative.

Anyway listening to that CD player would take up a lot of our days when we weren't washing dishes. Even on our days off, we would listen over and over again before it would get cold and dark and we would go inside to sleep to wake up for work the next morning. Music captivated us. I had been writing short stories and songs, primarily rap songs, for about 6-7 years. If it wasn't a rap song it was a story with some kind of killer in it that the school teacher would find and dismiss. I had written since I can remember. I still have songs I wrote when I was seven years old, two of which were called "Xcape" and "G-ride." I just started and never stopped. Writing was a strength of mine, or perhaps I should say storytelling. Before this I was occupied with being a kid, hanging with other kids trying to fuck girls, doing anything that was wrong, fun, and exciting.

But that summer, life slowed up. The environment kept moving around us with crime and poverty and struggle. We were honed in. I remember diving in head first in music studying every song and CD I possibly could. Studying cadence, rhythm, and delivery, whether it was rock, hip hop or R&B, or even country, which I also had an appreciation for. The outlaw shit. Willie, Waylon, Hank, Cash. Not the fake bullshit that would come post Dwight Yoakam. Luckily I was primarily exposed to the authentic shit. I had to listen to Leadbelly sing "Nobody Knows the Trouble I've Seen". After hearing that he carried a pistol, attempted to kill a man, went to prison and escaped, I really believed it. I wanted to listen to Mötley Crüe because they looked as crazy as they sounded and they lived as crazy as they looked. I listened to Sade when I wanted to hear a smooth voice. I loved Deftones and the Smashing Pumpkins because the "1979" video looked like our lives verbatim. I remember girls putting me onto Erykah Badu's *Baduizm* and Tori Amos' *Boys for Pele* and Fiona Apple's *Tidal* CD's and finding them in the pawn shops. A female vocal with a piano underneath is hypnotizing. These albums are still some of the best I've heard perhaps because I grew up with them and understand thoroughly every note. I turned even more introverted. Maybe I thought I had to discover who exactly I was going to be. We listened deliberately. Dissecting every song. I was positive nobody around me was feeling music the way I was. When I would listen to a song I was so sensitive to it I could feel it happening to me. This could be a really good thing or a painful ride to be on. No one around me seemed to be experiencing that same spell. Aside from that I was no longer running the road until the middle of the night getting into shit my mom would never believe. She had her own problems and run-ins with authority, plus she thought as mothers do that we could do no wrong. Anyway I could now sit with music sometimes for 16-18 hours on end just studying it. I never had another goal or dream as a kid. I never wanted to be a firefighter. Surely didn't want to be a cop. When I knew how to put pencil to paper I started writing songs and never stopped.

Later, journalists would ask me the typical question about music being that escape. The generic tale of the kid locked in his room with his radio playing and the posters on the wall rebelling against whatever his parents say, like the kid in the Twisted Sister video for "I Wanna Rock." But this wasn't me. This wasn't us. It wasn't that easy and it wasn't a choice where we could flip a switch and turn it off. We were city kids, not the typical white Middle America suburban angst-filled kids. You can shut your bedroom door and block the world out all you want but sometimes it gets kicked in by masked gunmen who have your mom at gunpoint for a DVD player. The boogeymen could find you under any occasion. So our skin was thick. If we were suffering we would do so in silence. If we were going to make it anywhere we would have to adapt to our surroundings, not live with our heads in the clouds. So I had to do both. Foremost I was obligated to ride out for any type of bullshit my friends or family were getting into and when that wasn't going down it was okay to work on music. I couldn't turn my back on anyone and I can't explain to them that music isn't an escape. It's difficult to convey the idea that performing songs isn't a purge of sorts rather it rips you apart on the inside every time and ends up ruining your day, week, month etc. That kind of horripilation test is how you know you have something good, something worthwhile. The part none of them talk about is how painful it is and how negative these things might be. They talk about purging and music being an outlet. They talk about being in bliss on stage and being liberated. None of them ever talk about how telling stories that rip you apart night after night on a stage for years on end can effect you. If we know attitude is everything and thoughts become words which become things imagine repeating these negative mantras every night in the form of songs. Imagine how this could effect your neuroplasticity. Of course this is a bit of a sadomasochistic choice but I don't hear many people touch on it. All I hear are the phrases people borrow and parrot and they don't feel very accurate to me. I think people mistake the attention and praise they receive from creating music with the idea of music being a purging outlet. To me that attention and praise may take a bit of the edge off but it only masks it temporarily. In no way is it long term effective or therapeutic.

A lot of people have some kind of impactful life experience that makes them turn a corner. Running away and moving out on your own, having to rough it while you pursue your goals. Or your parents getting divorced. Or getting arrested for the first time before vowing to become more focused in life and stay out of trouble. Petty stuff that rattles the cages of sheltered squares everywhere. The kind of self defining events you can hear either sex loudly boasting about from across the room in any shitty food and alcohol franchise in America. Some people, however, are met with adversity on a day to day basis. These kinds of people are special and sometimes become artists or experts, inspirational in whatever it is they do. They can be great contributors to society. Up to this point I had been arrested a dozen times for petty shit. Fighting or using a weapon on someone whether in school or out. Stealing from stores or houses. Kid shit. I had buried slain friends and family members. Had sex regularly, saw the effects that drugs had on people. By drugs I mean heroin, not weed. By effects I mean death. I witnessed someone die with the needle in their arm. I saw elementary kids shooting each other dead. I went to funerals where the casket remained closed because the kid had his head blown clean off or was set on fire. Yes. Set on fire.

My reality wasn't a game. Being homeless. Being hungry. Being on the run. I worry this book will end without me being able to articulate the pain it should contain. But it helped to cultivate a strong radar for bullshit and a real ability to read people and judge character. This is something school cannot teach you. This could also be called "street smarts" not in the way people refer to street smarts today which because of how insulated we've become more so just refers to common sense. Anyway having this kind of social awareness as a music listener was helpful too. Knowing how these situations played out having experienced them, I was drawn to music that struck an emotional nerve. Like some kind of ingrained litmus test. I have early memories of my dad playing Metallica and I thought that was catchy and cool but the kind of things I would first "feel" were hip hop and rap. When Scarface said calmly and in plain English "I never seen a man cry till I seen a man die," I get goosebumps even as I write this. A more light-hearted example would be the stories Bob Seger tells in his songs. Maybe I'm biased toward a fellow Michigan boy but he tells vivid stories that bring you right to the place and time he's talking about. These were the types of writers I wanted to be like. I had been hearing 2pac for years but around this point I started listening and understanding. When you focus on the message and transport yourself to the song's inception. Cross referencing artists and genres and finding similarities between them was a hobby I spent a good deal of time on. Bob Marley "I Shot the Sheriff" John Cash "Folsom Prison Blues" Queen "Bohemian Rhapsody" Snoop Dogg "Murder Was The Case" all very popular songs people know and love all about killing someone. The Eagles "Lyin' Eyes" Bill Withers "Who Is He (And What Is He To You)" Hank Williams "Your Cheatin' Heart" Chuck Berry "Maybellene" all about infidelity. Jimi Hendrix "Hey

Joe" Rammstein "Klavier" Eminem "Kim" all songs people know and love all about killing a cheating lover etc. R. Kelly "I Wish" Elton John "Candle In The Wind" Pete Rock & CL Smooth "When They Reminisce Over You (T.R.O.Y.)" Eric Clapton "Tears In Heaven" all reminiscing about the dead. I also noticed the suspension of disbelief starts when the melody begins.

I was probably too young to make the obvious call that we as humans only possess a few basic emotions. That everyone had a lot more in common than we thought. When it comes to writing songs you can't express the countless number of emotional variations. Or the endless number of scenarios people can get themselves into. It comes down to a handful of feelings or ideas to articulate and equivocate.

As a kid I wanted to be the best. I wanted to conjure up images so strong that the listener felt like they were there. I had experiences people didn't typically have. I knew these experiences well because they happened often. It's hard to recall exciting events when they happen to you once. When people try and put together the pieces of a past traumatic event, even one that just happened, you often get quotes like "it came out of nowhere" or "it all happened so fast." However when they happen often you gain a grip on them. Fighting is overly exciting to most people. But a professional fighter is trained to be calm and slow his heart. The same goes for an infantry man who has seen battle. Your first gun fight is loud and hectic and comes in flashes. Your tenth doesn't have the same effect. Situational awareness. You gain a level head. You're able to observe what's happening around you more accurately. If I wanted to make people feel my writing I would have to learn how to articulate, how to bring people where I had been.

As I got older this would be the difference between my writing and that of my peers. The way I saw it their knowledge and experience was thin. The things they talked about were fictional, therefore they were fake, as writers. I don't mean fiction as a genre. Fiction is the same as nonfiction in that the better you are at bringing your reader where you want them the better writer you are. This is used in character writing and all that bullshit commonly used in heavy music. But I'm speaking about the ability to convey emotion. What I mean is the anger isn't genuine, the experience didn't happen, the emotion is a contrived reiteration of the work of someone they admire, the love isn't real, the pain never existed and the attitude is an act, FICTION. This is not to mention anything of success. Music is a charlatan's game and these musicians who more resemble psychics than specialists get rewarded just the same. As we know in today's world it's easy for the conman pulling on the heart strings to earn better living than the brain surgeon. But I hadn't made this observation then. At this point my thinking was that having access to that kind of vault of experiences works almost as a toolbox. It will always be there no matter how your reality changes. The past has a permanent residency you can never take away. This would alienate me and my group in the future but more about that later, I was still washing dishes 10 hours a day.

The job was becoming uninteresting. Being someone who talked little and watched a lot I had a few key observations about work. I remember wondering why I as a teenager had the same job a 50 year old man had. At this time I didn't have any economic knowledge or sociological theories under my belt but I knew something was amiss. I didn't see myself in any of these people. My friends, the kids I grew up around in the street, these were the people I respected. My older friends had cars and girls and things they wanted. These workers wanted the same things but were 20 years older and still got rides to work, were single and complained constantly about what they didn't have. When I looked down the dish line at the backs of the cooks while they made orders I imagined myself ten or twenty years older in this same job. I couldn't see it. I continue to use this visualization as an adult, always considering the opinion of my teenage self when making decisions. I had to quit. I decided to always consider the opinion of my child self.

In hindsight I realize this is a bit of an unfair analogy. I wanted to touch on this ideology because I hear it repeated by young people and adults alike and I feel like it's a narrow idea that is very wrong yet never questioned. In this context the choice people have is not work or hustle the end. Although people try to interpret the world like its black or white these things like most things are nuanced. The people I worked with which represent the prototypical working man in this story but not in every story are a one sided sample. For example the owner of the franchise who had the Mercedes Benz and the girls and the gold chains just like the successful hustlers I knew also worked in the shitty Coney Islands as a kid. Nobody put him on. The people who ran his several restaurants did as well. They worked hard and got themselves into position to run their own businesses. The people I worked with made poor choices from morning to night. Their lives were hell. They don't tell the whole story. One of many ways this thinking is off is because it doesn't take into account all the unsuccessful hustlers we all know. The ones who fuck up every sack they get and pay the money back. The ones who still get rides to middle man plays and can never get ahead who complain alike. The ones who fuck up and start using and become junkies. The ones who are killed as well because death is no success. When Biggie said, "either you're slangin' crack rock or you got a wicked jump shot," he may have been accurate in 1994 but these types of insights don't seem to get updated with the times. This was before the days where entrepreneurial minors could build multi million dollar companies from their bedrooms. The facts are the odds of getting into the NBA if you make it to a college senior are 1 in 75 or 1.3%. That's a 98.7% failure rate. The odds of becoming a successful drug dealer and getting away clean and free as we know are even less. Starting your own business you have a 30% chance of failure in the first 2 years and a 50% chance of failure in the first five years and when that fails you can continue trying. These odds are exponential. The accessibility of the internet, its information and resources has created a countless number of fortunes. This is not my career advice column and that is not to say there are not challenges. I come from a place that is known across the world for its problems and this is not what I did with my life which you will soon learn but it is harmful for those who know better not to educate the younger generations so they understand they are in control and have some tools out there. There are people out there that directly oppress people but a more subtle form of oppression is not educating those who look up to you. I think in summary there is another point worth making that most people over look and that is not to make assumptions about things or people based on the very little experience you have with it. There is an idea that says reading one book on a subject will make you 50% more knowledgeable about a topic than the rest of the world and reading three books on a subject will leave you 95% more informed on a subject than the rest of the world, etc., you get the idea. One problem with this idea is it's just a telling study of people in the world. A bigger problem with it is that people mistake knowing about something with experiencing the world in practice. Anyone who watches a video of someone changing the brakes on their car then attempts to do so themselves knows where this leads. The truth is you can find a 'how to' on mostly anything you can imagine, but it doesn't mean anything. I brought this up to get to a point about experience. If people believe the above idea about reading something then it stands ten fold about experiencing something. People constantly make assumptions and judgements based on either a quick Google search or "their experience" with something which is usually a very lacking anomaly experience. They also build mountains of ideology upon their knowledge of persons or a people based on their minority one off experiences. Thus the age of the armchair expert i.e. the modern jackass. Since I didn't know any of this at the time lets get back to my own ignorance.

I worked this job for only a little while before I couldn't force myself to do it anymore and hand my shirts off to Yon. He would replace me. All I did was daydream about music and the future at work anyway. I didn't care about money. Quitting meant being hungry but I didn't care about that either. I had tunnel vision and it wouldn't take long for me to realize I had to stop working and become proactive about writing. The most exciting things we did at Angelo's aside from trying to fuck the owner's daughter was finding a dead guy in the men's bathroom. A man who had a heart attack, rather. I think he died later but when we found him he was only "on his way". This reminds me of the first dead body I stumbled upon.

A couple years prior I was on the east side with a few friends. I had ran off to the store and saw a guy laying on the side of the road. Although by this age I had shot a few guns, understood people were killing each other around me, saw a few people in caskets, knew what death was and how it worked, I also knew plenty homeless slept in the street so I didn't think this guy was dead. There was no blood or bullets on the scene, his head wasn't blown off. For all I knew he was wasted and passed out. His face was down in the crevice where the curb meets the street. An odd place to fall asleep I thought. I don't know why I didn't leave him alone and mind my business. I probably thought he was drunk and passed out and I could steal something off him. He was still. No one was around so I nudged the back of his head with my foot trying to see his face. Don't know why I cared. No blood, but it was clear he was dead. I remembered being arrested a few years back for an assault. I didn't want to get arrested again so I took off. Later on I wrote a couple lines about it in a song called "War Outside": *"Seen my first body when I was a kid. I thought sleeping in streets was just something they did. Then I got older I never grew up. I wouldn't let them take something I didn't get enough of."* Subscribing to the possibility that I had been robbed of a typical childhood and I still chased that fantasy. What's typical anyway?

After I quit working I went back home and continued being a kid. This meant listening to music all day and only stopping to go to the CD store to steal more discs to study. When this wasn't happening there was a mail order company called BMG you could order a handful of CD's from without paying. We changed the name and information on the order forms so many times they flagged our address and would no longer send CD's to our house at which point we would send them to our friend's house. When that didn't fly we sent them to abandon houses and waited for them. If I had to guess I would say our group combined probably finessed about 1000 discs from them. Good looks. It was almost right on cue that after spending a summer in a trance listening to music my brother would bring a friend over who turned out to be our cousin. His name was Kat and he played an instrument. Drums. We didn't know anyone that played an instrument at this time. We wanted in.

Around age 6 I thought I would be a writer. When I found rap music I imagined I was to become a rapper. When I met people that played instruments I would become a frontman. These were all the same to me.

Kat would school us on how music worked. He would talk about bars and notes and have us tapping out drum beats for hours When I say tapping out I mean hitting your knees with your hands and stomping your feet on the floor. Kat was a guy obsessed with music but he was another poor fucker like we were with a shitty family and shitty upbringing. Played the drums but didn't have a drum set. But he did have a dream so he fit right in. As I mentioned before my CD collection consisted of diverse things like Master P *Ghetto D* and DMX *It's Dark and Hell is Hot*. Kat's consisted of Slipknot, Pantera, and and Alice in Chains. At this point we made the decision we were all in on forming a band. So without instruments or money to buy them we assigned positions. I thought mine was fairly simple, I asked Kat, "Do you think we're going to need microphones at all? I'm gonna be screamin' pretty loud." We had a long way to go.

We would spend days talking about our look. Our album and the way it would sound. The names of the songs. We spoke about touring with Slipknot and having fire all over our stage like Rammstein and smashing our gear like Trent Reznor does in the *Closure* VHS. We would plan out our stage show and our costume changes like Marilyn Manson but have 100 people on stage like Wu Tang Clan. We would draw pictures instead of doing school work and write out lyrics to Tool songs like we understood them and also write some of our own. We would type out live show plans and interviews with journalists that didn't exist. We would arrange furniture like a stage and "perform" whole concerts of cover songs in our basement for no one all day. This came complete with a goth phase where we would walk around looking like "The Crow." We thought we had to look the part.

The summer would fade out just as quickly as it came on us. This time we weren't moving anywhere though. We were staying in Flint for good. When we started school it became clear this was the last place we belonged. School and goth don't really go hand in hand. Everybody's favorite rappers had yet to wear dresses while donning multi color hair and facial tattoos and piercings. We were a bit ahead of the curve so we were not accepted. The only people to embrace us in school were a bunch of girls which we took full advantage of. At the time we didn't understand that these young girls had a complex and were drawn to us as a result of their own oppressive environment but who cares. I fought a lot.

Since being jumped as a kid I had been in more fights than I can recall. I started either getting suspended every week or just not going which was what I had been doing the past few years with my mom. School out at my dad's didn't bother me. It was in the country and much different. It was easy not to attend school in Flint. The school knew not to try and call my mom or the parents of my friends. They didn't get very far doing so. They had a designated guy at the school who would take us home. He would drop us off and we would walk around the neighborhood reciting lyrics to songs we liked. I remember racking up so many detention hours that it was impossible for me to complete them if I went every day until the end of the school year. At this point I would be expelled with a few of my friends, and Kat.

4

Let Me Be Alone

School wasn't for me. I never wanted anything it had to offer. To this day I don't have a single high school credit. I had been trying to drop out of school since the 6th grade at McKinley middle school. This was a school similar to the movie Dangerous Minds with Michelle Pfeiffer. The kind of school you walk through a metal detector to get into and the teachers didn't do much teaching. There were guns and drugs which I was indifferent to. Smoking cigarettes or fucking girls in the bathroom was the best way to cut class in the 6th grade. The whole thing kind of got old though. I always thought ahead about what I wanted to be doing and school was never a part of my plan. I wasn't positive about the means in which I would achieve what I wanted but I do remember listening to and reciting lines like Biggie's "Cuz GED wasn't BIG I got PAID that's why my mom hates me" so I knew school wasn't a necessity. Plus with my mom not being around much there was no one to keep the pressure on. The value of school was never stressed. Everyone I knew dropped out. My parents didn't finish school and my brothers and sisters hadn't either. I never had it in my head that I would finish. That wasn't my vision. So it was only a matter of time.

I didn't know it then but thinking back on it now it was everyone's transparency that demystified a lot of authority figures growing up, whether it was parents or police or teachers. I think it's the same way for a lot of kids in underprivileged areas. The roles weren't well defined for us. I would break down these barriers one day when missing the bus and waiting in the parking lot before walking home. Probably because home was the last place I wanted to be. I sat on the bleachers watching the teachers get into their cars and leave one by one. Maybe I was waiting for them to offer a ride, I don't know. Anyway, I noticed their cars weren't new or in nice condition. I knew a few kids who had nicer cars than these, I thought to myself. These were regular people. When they spoke despairingly about their spouse to the class it was because they were unhappy. When they fell asleep while we were taking a test it was because they were bored. When they left work they didn't necessarily drive their dream car home to their ideal life. These were the people educating us. They went to college and got a degree, for this. I didn't care for teachers mostly because several of them told me I would just end up in jail or in a gang and asked me often why I was wasting their time. I guess they weren't too far off so I don't hold it against them. On top of this there was never anything in them I admired. They weren't role model figures worth looking up to. They resembled a peer group I didn't associate with more than they resembled leaders.

When I decided to go to the first and only detention I would ever attend it was a female supervisor. She was present while everyone sat quietly and waited for the couple hours to be up. I sat at a little table inside the cubicle off to her right. I don't know if she ever knew I was there because I don't think she could see me unless she leaned back and looked and I was pretty quiet. Anyway, she was trying to quietly have some kind of phone sex on her cell phone as the detention started. Kids were talking and carrying on but I heard her talk about a bunch of nasty shit she apparently had done or planned on doing with the guy or girl on the other end of the line. This kept my attention and sparked a bunch of ideas and really gave me some whole new game but after she hung up the phone 15 minutes into the detention I grew impatient and left.

My final day at school came not long after that. I didn't do anything outside of the norm on this particular day. I only appeared in school when I had some girlfriends to see or when Yon wanted me there. This had me attending about a week of school a month. A day here and a day there. I fought or skipped or walked the halls doing nothing. They probably saw this as one of their few opportunities to catch up with me. With my busy schedule and all. I went in and sat with the principal. He explained to me that he was expelling me for the year and that I couldn't come back the following year either. He then explained I shouldn't bother coming back to his school at all. I had racked up so many detention hours in the short time I had been there that if I served detention every day for the rest of the year, I still wouldn't be able to complete the hours I owed. I also never did one assignment or project and didn't participate in anything. I took this as a legitimate free pass out of school. The man who drove us home asked me which house he should take me to. I told him to take me to the neighborhood and drop me off. Finally.

I wouldn't miss anything about school. I played football all through middle school into high school and had some good stats. I was good at the game. A few of the kids I played with would go to the NFL and I probably could have too had I stuck with it. But I wasn't taught how the school system worked. I didn't know you could do well and get scholarships and grants. It sounds ignorant to say but I was textbook stupid. I had no clue what you did in school could change your whole life. I also had no one around me that could put me up on game but I don't blame anybody. I damned myself from the beginning. I would never know shit about a graduation or a prom or a class reunion. I was never on a list for good grades or good performance of any kind. Oh well. My attitude nowadays is more that school is important for socializing a child but not a prerequisite for success or necessary to acquire knowledge. That could be luck that I landed in a progressive time when this was true or becoming true. Ten years earlier would've been less true and twenty years earlier even less so. Whatever.

This was around the time most kids were diving heavy into drugs, graduating from smoking cigarettes and drinking alcohol and weed to the harder shit like the pills, coke and heroin my class-mates were shooting each other over. This still didn't phase me. At this age I was hardened and desensitized. Maybe because I had to be. Maybe because everyone around me was always hysterical or irate or falling apart over something. Maybe because my mother always looked to me for strength. Because those around me were weak I had to be strong at all times even when I wasn't. I had no problem resisting drugs before this and nothing was different now. Even when I knew through their songs that most of the musicians I was paying attention to were on drugs and my friends and family were on drugs they just didn't appeal to me. As a kid there was nothing attractive about them. There was no temptation. As a teenager maybe another reason came into play. There was still nothing attractive about them but on top of that I had seen several people die or get killed over them. Death didn't bother me. I was indifferent to the dying process but obsessed with my own death. A large part of me was drawn and attracted to the lifestyle. The lifestyle I heard about in music. The lifestyle I had seen play out around me. However I knew I wasn't going to let anyone kill me so maybe that's why. I needed to stay focused. This may seem like an exaggerated state of mind but this is how I conditioned myself to think. Even at a young age I vividly remember myself taking everything much too seriously than I should have. It probably robbed me of some good times.

School and drugs aside, we now attempted to practice music as a group. Practice meant makeshift drum kits in the back yard and pounding on them. The kinds of drum kits made from five gallon buckets and tires that you played with plastic coat hangers. My aunt next door would occasionally spy on us and scold us for swearing in our songs. It was safe to say we didn't have the necessary gear to be a functional band but we were deep in music and dreaming about fame and fortune. Kat had a lot of answers.

Unbeknownst to us, the internet existed. We had heard of this thing before but had no clue what it was or how it worked. In the nineties this was a shell of what it is today. We were too poor to afford a PC but the libraries had them and Kat taught us how to use them to find information, which we wanted a lot of. This became one of our two primary activities this particular year. Going to the library to use their internet capable computers for 15 minutes to a half an hour. If no one signed in on the sheet after you, you could sign your name twice and use a whole hour of internet before your log in was invalid for the day. At this point we would get up and walk to the next library across town. Each one was about an hour away from the next and it wasn't unusual for us to hit three in a day. This was the equivalent to studying music in the broken down car in the driveway. Only this car had thousands of books and computers and a seemingly infinite amount of information. Different librarians had different rules, some didn't care at all and some took their jobs very seriously. The downtown library was the biggest with the most computers and the highest time limits. It was also the most comfortable. It had large rooms with high ceilings full of bookshelves and tables you could sit and read at. It was a couple stories and there were even private rooms you could go into to read or write, etc. It was an hour and a half walk but it was worth it. The internet was a whole new world from the library computers which used to just contain a handful of games for kids. Learning games and Oregon Trail and things like that. This was something different. Most bands we knew of didn't even have websites. But we would spend hours looking up photos of groups and unreleased interviews that were probably fake. Naturally when this grew tiring we would have to slide into primitive chat rooms where we would try to get girls' phone numbers and meet up with them which almost never happened. It wasn't unusual for us to be spending eight hours or more in the big library. There were so many different computer rooms and levels that we could always catch someone who only used their log for 15 minutes and sit in on the remainder of their hour. Of course, some people were better at this than others, so this rendered a few of us here and there wandering around the library which wasn't as bad as some of the hang out spots I otherwise had.

Being a teenager from Flint makes you an adult. As we all know this doesn't mean we're fully developed beings from a biological or psychological stand point. But we can be tried as adults for murder so we take the good with the bad and consider ourselves grown. Having done the bulk of my maturing before being introduced into an environment completely submerged in "the network" is important to consider. Being one of the last if not the last generation on the cusp of the technology age makes us ignorant or naive to the whole "technology culture". This is a strange culture because it doesn't have a centralized geographical origin, it exists all across the world. It would be several years before the internet would become what it is today, but we always had to earn it. I would parallel this to primitive cultures who didn't have access to resources within their homes. If we wanted to spend an hour on the computer we had to walk an hour to the computer and an hour back. If we wanted to read a book we had to walk an hour to the book and an hour back. Technology wasn't at our fingertips until much later in life and we certainly were not afforded many luxuries.

When the computer time ran out I would spend my day reading. I could read a whole book in one sitting. I would find a handful of books and sitting at the table with them anything left over at the end of the day I would borrow and take home. I always wanted to be smarter and more educated. There was nothing appealing to me about being ignorant. I was attracted to the biggest books. I figured they contained the most information. I remember reading things like *Bulfinche's Mythology* and biographies of important people in history whom which I would hear about in the songs I listened to. I soon learned I didn't like biographies even about people I assumed I admired. Perhaps because it killed my own imagination or I was so hungry for knowledge that a look into someone else life was useless to me. I thought it worth mentioning I've not researched how a book like the one you're currently reading should be written. Anyway I switched my focus to psychology, sociology and poetry. My favorite novel was and still is *Niels Lyhne* by Danish author Jens Peter Jacobsen. When I imagine a handful of my favorite passages from that book I am embarrassed of my own prose as I write this.

I think what I liked most about books was each offered a real life victory. One you could quantify. One that validated you. I could drop out of school as a kid and give them reasons why. I had read *Lies My Teacher Told Me* by James Loewen. I could pull stories and facts about American history. But that didn't get very far with anyone. They had grown up believing something and they took it as the truth. I sounded like a misinformed kid that had read some bullshit somewhere. If I read somewhere that the world was evolving save for the field of education, I might get a raised eyebrow. If I explained that explicit knowledge or factoid memorization, championed by the education industrial complex, will give you a high score in Trivial Pursuit before it'll earn you a Nobel Peace Prize. Or that tacit understanding is a procedural knowledge more difficult to pass along through words or writing. I could then align myself with likeminded figures from the past. This is what I liked about reading. In a few hours I could devour a book that would summarize an idea that would otherwise take months or years to cultivate on my own. To me this meant the more I read and understood what I read the more it would force me to evolve. My competitive side kicked in. Another book I found was *Letters to a Young Poet* by Rainer Maria Rilke. This was a bible to me. When a younger poet asks Rilke for his opinion on his poems, he says:

"You ask whether your verses are any good. You ask me. You have asked others before this. You send them to magazines. You compare them with other poems, and you are upset when certain editors reject your work. Now (since you have said you want my advice) I beg you to stop doing that sort of thing. You are looking outside, and that is what you should most avoid right now. No one can advise or help you — no one. There is only one thing you should do. Go into yourself. Find out the reason that commands you to write; see whether it has spread its roots into the very depths of your heart; confess to yourself whether you would have to die if you were forbidden to write. This most of all: ask yourself in the most silent hour of your night: must I write? Dig into yourself for a deep answer. And if this answer rings out in assent, if you meet this solemn question with a strong, simple "I must," then build your life in accordance with this necessity; your while life, even into its humblest and most indifferent hour, must become a sign and witness to this impulse."

This was the wisdom I had been seeking and I applied it to everything. I wasn't interested in fictional characters. I was interested in real life, and obtainable talent and greatness. Although there is great utility in fictions especially the classics I saw myself as an urgent case and needed something stat. I sought wisdom because those around me were unwise. Now I understand that even if I were surrounded by great teachers in life I wouldn't have learned a thing until I decided to be taught. Beyond that receiving the knowledge was just the first step. It took several years before I was able to assimilate the information and extract the ideas and offer them perspective and context which is just as important as the discovery process. Possessing this skill equips you with a hyper awareness that facilitates a quicker understanding of information and ideas. Especially when you start adapting concepts across different fields of study. It bears repeating that study is no replacement for practice and experience. I needed to have both which is why adults don't listen to children.

The library was a sort of sanctuary. Nothing would happen to us while we were there. It was quiet and peaceful. The people that worked there were kind. We weren't interested in what was happening outside that building. And I didn't feel like we were missing anything. We were locked in.

After six or eight hours we would get hungry. We would run to the nearest party store and steal a jar of peanut butter or something like it and take turns scooping handfuls of it out until we were full. I wasn't the most hip in the group to the internet thing. Or technology period. I thought it was useful for information or communications and still do but I wasn't the best at navigating around one or typing, etc. Years down the line when Facebook came I wouldn't bother with one of those. I had read *Brave New World*. I knew how the shit ends. I wouldn't even get a cell phone until I was 20 years old. I believe it was called a Razor. I would keep reading a habit and completed a book a week minimum.

My philosophies formed over the years. These were the kind of underdeveloped ideas kids have. I felt like I knew something everyone else didn't. Like I had access to genius and all I had to do was show up. Information didn't cost a dime. It became an obsession. I wanted to know everything. I wanted to do everything, at any costs, regardless of who stood in the way. We became a group obsessed. We went to sleep thinking about one thing. We woke up thinking about it. All our minor goals and activities only complemented our single major interest. This was long before I had discovered what psychologist Anders Ericsson calls "deliberate practice."

When we weren't soaking up information we were stealing shit. This is the only way we could get all the equipment we needed to be a real band. We didn't have a pot to piss in. Some days we slept outside. Some days we had no heat or electricity. A lot of days we had no food. But this isn't about that. One day we needed an Iron Cobra double bass pedal. This is what all the rock bands had and they were two hundred dollars. We would have to take one from the store. Me and Kat walked up to the music store with a drum key. We would need this to take the connector bar off the pedals to break it down and make it easier. Thinking back on it these guys had to have known what we were up to. We looked like bums off the street. We went in the store every other day and never bought a thing, we never even talked to them about gear. We just had our checklist of necessary pieces of gear and were here to do some stealing. The drum room was in the back of the store. When no one was watching I detached the connecter bar and mallets and handed them to Kat who pocketed them along with the key. I had already mentally rehearsed this a hundred times at home. The trickiest part would be to rip the pedals from the Velcro without making a noise. The inspiration that sat in the back of my mind was always about Sublime. If Brad Nowell could steal a guitar from a pawn shop in the LA riots I could do this. I slowly tore the pedals off while Kat talked over it and looked out. This took what seemed like several minutes. I sat them on the floor next to the row of pedals so they didn't stand out in anyway and stood up and continued walking around looking at cymbals. The hard part was done. When the coast was clear I slid the pedal plates down my pants one at a time letting the castings catch on my waist band to prevent them from falling down my pant leg. I threw my shirt over the protruding pieces. Of course there was a bulge in my stomach region but I didn't care. I had the pedals and I was ready to run for it if I had to. I walked out toward the door calmly and right as I was getting to the exit one of the heavier set guys that worked there yelled, "Hey what do you have?!" Me and Kat went to plan B and ran as he gave chase. We ran out into a busy road full of traffic disrupting the flow of cars like you see in the movies. A few blocks down the road and we were in a garage relishing in our victory. The realization that we had no bass drum to hook it up to didn't matter, this just meant we had to steal one.

This became the basic pattern from store to store. Sometimes it would involve walking an hour to a pawn shop. Pawn shops kept the drum stuff in the back too. On several occasions I remember going in and taking two and three pairs of hi hat cymbals at a time in my pants. Sometimes we could go undetected and get away and sometimes we would get chased. We ended up with dozens of 14" hi hats we also used for crash cymbals because that was all we were working with.

Our mom saw how serious we were about this and did her best to help in buying us things here and there. My mom was with a chick at the time although she assumed none of us noticed this woman who I'll call Meisha had played guitar and advised her on a purchase. She would show me some things when we would catch each other lying around the house. We compensated where she fell short by doin BE's and taking from people that had nice shit. Or stores that carried the stuff we wanted. This isn't supposed to be inspiration to steal or rob, of course you can do many things to solve your problem, but this is what I chose to do. I needed these things now because I swore we were going to blow up tomorrow. I would be damned if I was going to turn out like all the would be rock stars or rappers you would see bum around town and make excuses about their circumstances. The ones that were one scenario away from "hitting it big" when in reality they only played a few shitty shows at the local bar. As I said before we were all in, there was no secondary interest. We were going to go hard regardless of the consequences until we had professional gear like the pros had and then some, of course to smash onstage.

Storytelling in our culture revolves around the childhood hero. Whether the work is fiction or non-fiction, a novel or a memoir. The hero is typically capable of impossible things on a daily basis. This story doesn't have much of that. Admittedly I held several people in high esteem through the years but even as a kid I remember having a very black and white mind set. There were only two kinds of people. People that were making my life better and people that were making it worse. I ranked and prioritized them accordingly. I recall cutting off family and friends coldly if they didn't believe in me which none of them did. I didn't blame them or give it a second thought at all. They did upset me at the time to a degree but I knew I had no reason to be around them. At this point I had been so let down I didn't expect anything from anyone and not much got to me. We believed in each other as a crew and when crew stopped believing they were marginalized as well. In hindsight we probably looked like a group of confused stupid kids and we were. I decided when someone tells you you can't do something they really mean they can't do it.

That being said at this point it was as if we were masterless apprentices. We would spend all our time either at the library or practicing playing the gear we were slowly accumulating. We were uninterested in anything else. We even conducted recording sessions. Now you can do these things from your bedroom but back then we had to use the answering machine as a recording device. If we put the loud percussive things we were pounding on far away from the machine and placed anything with strings that was quiet near the machine and put the vocal which was kind of loud somewhere between the two "instruments" we could achieve something like a pop mix recording of 30 seconds of an original song of ours. Which would captivate us for months. It didn't necessarily get our mom a job when potential employers called and got our recordings on the answering machines with a bunch of "fuck you's" in there, but we didn't care. We would spend all day making songs this way and thinking of new ones and recording over the old one. I don't know why we just didn't find more tapes and start a catalogue.

Nothing came easy to us. The world pushed and pulled us like a tide when we let it. When we were focused it was as if our feet were planted in the sand but when we let our guard down it would carry us where it wanted. It would expose us to the real world. Back to the neighborhood where it was a gang encounter or a fist fight or a robbery or a shootout or a party or a murder or HIV, another boogeyman. A few people I knew had caught the germ. I remember being scared of it as a kid. Not scared enough not to have unprotected sex, of course, but paranoid about it after the fact. Anytime I didn't use a condom I assumed immediately that I had caught HIV. I still recall my first paranoia spell which lasted almost a year.

It was cold and rainy. I was soaking wet, I decided once I got into the city from the township I would hop on the bus and get home quicker because it was late 9 or 10 at night or whatever and I had a dollar. I sat in the bus stop and waited and the bus came. I got on the bus and there was a chick I knew from school there. Her name was Keisha. She was a neighborhood hoe. We were the same age. Anyway, I always notice people but they don't notice me so I go to the back of the empty bus and sit. A minute or two passes and she gets up and moves to the back of the bus to sit across from me. We talk about whatever kids talk about for five minutes or so and she asks if she can get off at my stop which was only about a mile from the downtown bus station. I told her yeah but we had to be quiet and we had to hang out in the basement. I explained that its likely no one would be home but if anyone were home it would be my ma's crazy boyfriend whom I would have to fight. His daughters I consider my sisters but these fights ended often in broken bones from small things like fingers, hands and feet ranging to more serious injuries like the time I dealt him a broken back. I explained to her it was his crib and all that. We got to my stop, hopped off the bus, and I sneak her downstairs. We end up fuckin' after a minute or two of talking and afterward she's kind of in a hurry. She asks if I need any money and I say yeah so she gives me 20 dollars and asks if it's enough. I said yeah and she left, I assume to get back on the bus or to walk to the station, etc. I thought that was pretty cool for a few days. I had no idea why she thought I needed money. Maybe because of the condition of my house. I was riding the bus a few weeks later and we ended up on the same bus again. I thought maybe the same thing could go down but when I sat next to her she told me this story.

She said that night we hooked up she was going to meet her boyfriend at the bus station. Apparently because of our rendezvous she kept him waiting an hour so he fucked her up. Then she pulled open her coat and shirt and showed me that he had cut her with a razor all over her arms, chest, and stomach, probably about a dozen cuts 6-8 inches long everywhere. I don't know if she was telling the truth or she had seen me so she decided to pin it on me but the story seemed to make sense. I haven't seen her since. My bad homegirl.

5

Wolves

The struggle always seemed to make itself known. Whether the memory is a good one or a bad one. Whether we were happy or sad. Whether we were living or dying. We tried to keep it contained. Outwardly appearing to be unaffected but every minute of every day I recall a storm would brew inside me. If the old adage "ignorance is bliss" is true then what does the other side look like? Perhaps it's safe to say that the more a person knows, the more he or she can observe and comprehend about any given situation, the more one can be acquainted with pain. To experience it more intimately and to know it deeper as well. Beyond the simplicity of pain as a physical sensation like the kind you feel when a bullet tears your skin open and climbs inside you. Beyond the seemingly simple mental reaction to pain that you might experience when you watch the strongest person you know cry herself to sleep because she can't do Christmas this year. I mean a complex type of chronic pain with a root system that has worked its way into your body and mind and in those around you and through the streets of your neighborhood and throughout your city and even worse through time across the generations of your family leading up to you here and now as you continue to feed it so it may be passed on.

A few years later I was still a teenager. My mom had a house and
it was just us dozen kids and her. But mostly us because she was
either working or in jail or we had no idea where or for how long.
A handful of these were these same friends. The lifestyle doesn't
facilitate acquaintances. If you're in, you're all the way in. Maybe
because we were living so low you had to really trust the next
guy because being around him meant he would sooner or later
be involved in whatever it was you would get into, which could
range anywhere from something stupid and petty to a life or death
situation. It isn't the typical get older and grow apart because of a
job or career or go off to college or get a girlfriend or have a kid or
any other excuse squares typically have. Our loyalty to each other
over the years has grown into a thing I imagine a battalion has in
common. We were still sharing the same bed, food, girlfriends,
living the same struggle, down to do whatever had to be done for
the next guy. It's very tough to have any kind of ego in this environment. So we would keep the group intact, adding guys we would
come across along the way, subtracting the guys that passed away
or just up and disappeared.

In addition to the library we had discovered a new facility in our
search for knowledge and access, a local music venue. This was
a small hall that held shows Fridays, Saturdays and sometimes
Sundays. Over time we got to know the staff and volunteered our
help doing whatever needed to be done around the venue. This
was real progress. After a few years we were offered a rehearsal
space in the basement of the venue. One where we could store our
gear and practice any hour of the day or night. We wouldn't be
stuck in house or the yard anymore. We would walk miles to our
practice space which was a little room in the basement of the hall.

We couldn't pay the rent for the space but we had an arrangement. We worked at the venue doing anything we could to learn about music and sound and how everything went in exchange for the space rent every month. Some days we would practice 10-12 hours through the day and night, only getting a sense of time when we would be scolded for practicing during a show in which case we would retire for the time being and try to lure girls downstairs into our space, which most often worked.

This was the place I met most of the musicians I know today. We came across Gene, a 6' 6" black dude with long dreads who lived on the east side. We had a few friends in common so I saw him around before getting to know him. I would go up to his school, Central High, during their lunch to hang out with girl(s). Gene was as crazy looking as we were with similar ambition so it was just a short time before we worked him into the fold. He was down. He invited me to come play guitar with his group and I said I would if I could bring Kat. Their drummer wasn't too good but the rest of the guys T, Nando and Munro I knew them from around the venue so it was fun for the time being. Kat and I played our first show with them. This was only about three years after we had started beating on pots and pans in the yard. I remember the show sounded like shit. We looked like shit. We took forever to set up. We played on the floor in front of the stage. There were a lot of people there because we had accumulated a lot of friends through the music scene not because we were any good. I did most of the thing with my back to the crowd because I had no clue what to do, then we went crazy and broke a bunch of our own shit. I've read a lot of stories about that high you get the first time you step on stage. I didn't get any of that in the slightest. It was uncomfortable and confusing at best. Then as quick as it started it was over with.

Shows gave us a different perspective. We never had an older role model to consult about music. We observed as much as possible and watched a lot. The road we were on suddenly became much longer when we saw real functional groups that were further along on the path than we were. These were mature adults with top of the line equipment and cohesive songs and sometimes just the 5 or 6 of us that worked the club were present for their shows. The technical aspect of live performance and gear was a slight reality check but we kept our eyes open and studied. We watched every band whether their sound appealed to us or not and learned from them. What worked live and what didn't. What gear was nice and what wasn't our style. What the crowd responded to and what got lost on them.

I remember a realization I had one night while watching a band play. The guys were older. Perhaps in their 40's. As they played for an audience of ten people I thought of the coney island and the worn out men who were the same age flipping burgers for an audience of ten customers. I pondered this for hours. This wouldn't be me.

When the shows would end and everyone would pack up and go home we would haul all of our gear up the stairs to the stage. Around midnight or one am we would set up and tear down and time ourselves for efficiency. We would then play full sets over and over again. When we ran out of songs we played cover songs, sometimes playing for 6-8 hours and going into the morning, playing for a completely empty room. Having no idea how to use the club PA this is something we would mess with for a while before figuring out. These sessions would go on until morning. After being up all night and hauling gear both ways we usually slept in our space. We did this a few days a week and never missed a show for several years.

Naturally my mom wanted to move out of the house we had been in for only a couple months. We saw this as an opportunity to be on our own. I convinced her to leave the house to me and my boys which she had no problem doing. She didn't mind because she had the house and bills in some other guy's name anyway.

After a few shows with the group I wasn't feeling it as much anymore. I think I wanted more control. I left the band to front one Yon had formed with T. All of these bands shared the same practice space. All the musicians constantly moved from group to group. T would eventually leave and make room for Sneek to join up with me and Yon.

Sneek was from a small town outside of Flint. We met downtown. He would get thrown out of his house or run away and come live in the slums with us. When my mom was home we would hide him in the basement, sometimes for days on end. When she moved out he could come out of hiding. Although he was supposed to be in school, he was down for whatever we got into so he was on the team. We played the Local as often as they would let us, usually once or twice a month. Trying to get the hang of it. We still weren't good at playing music together but the entertainment value of the live show was improving.

We would run out of food and money soon enough. Feeding ourselves became the daily task. One of our roommates knew a guy, Flynn, who worked at this Coney Island in the mall. He would hook us up with as much food as we wanted on the days he worked. We found out he was living in his truck in the mall parking lot with his friend Gar so we offered him a place to stay. It was a symbiotic relationship.

Flynn was a funny kid from the north side so I thought he was alright. He had an old Ford F150 Lariat pickup truck that sat in the driveway most days he wasn't working. It didn't take very long for our water to be shut off. But that didn't stop us much. When the water company comes and shuts your water off you just find someone to turn it back on. Everyone knows that guy with "the water tool." He shows up with a five or six foot long wrench usually in the back of some kind of pick-up truck. He takes the water cap out of your front lawn sticks the wrench down the pipe and twists. This kind of character can usually turn your electricity back on at the box or even cable at the telephone pole, for a small fee of course.

I don't recall whose idea it was but I remember one day we put a big tarp we had found in the bed of Flynn's truck. We hauled buckets of water from the spigot to the now sealed truck bed and dumped water in until it was full creating some kind of makeshift pool. This is where we would chill and float around. It wasn't the largest of pools and it probably wasn't too good for the shocks on the vehicle. Especially when we would jump off the porch into the shallow 2 feet of water. You might have guessed our goal was to get neighborhood girls in our "pool." They most always wrote us off as crazy but this stands out in my memory as a happy day. It was only a matter of time before the water department showed up again and this time for good. They removed the water cap from the lawn and filled the hole with cement. We admitted defeat and lived without running water.

The electricity was the next to get cut off. We also had no food when Flynn wasn't working. A couple of us held jobs. A couple of us were too young to work. Most of us made our way stealing. This didn't always turn out as planned. Sometimes we would get caught. Sometimes shot at. Sometimes return with nothing at all. You couldn't count on much. After a while the house would turn into a real disgusting sight. When the neighbors weren't home we took buckets of water from their spigots. We would use this to drink and bathe and flush the toilets. But when your water service is cut off, you can only fill the back of the toilet with water to flush it so many times. Soon the pipes start backing up and fill the toilets and the basement with shit and piss. The mice, rats, bed bugs, ticks and lice came with it. Then the cockroach infestation came. At night before going to sleep or if I were having a girl over I remember having to brush the bed off and shake the blankets out to rid them of live maggots. None of this phased me really. I had slept in cars and motels and stranger's houses growing up it didn't bother me but some girls just didn't play that shit. I would learn over the years that if a girl will sleep in a bed of maggots with you, you gotta stick with her.

Of course it wasn't the ideal life but as long as we had food and a place to rehearse we were okay. The only problem was we started to run out of food and our water supplies starting seizing up. The rent for the rehearsal space was going up and our gear was breaking

and needed to be fixed or replaced. The walls seemed to be clos-
ing in on us. It took a while of grinding it out before crossing the
threshold and deciding that I personally no longer wanted to live
without water and electricity and food and clothes.

No one was coming to bail us out. Our parents either weren't
around or doing just as bad or worse. At this time, minimum wage
was $5.15. If we all had jobs I'm sure we could've made it work.
It's important to understand the state of the economy in my city.
Sometimes I went to other towns and saw signs in the windows
of fast food chains advertising one or two days a week where they
host walk-in interviews. This doesn't happen in Flint. Jobs aren't
plentiful. Crime has been high since the late 80's when GM pulled
80,000 jobs out of a city with roughly 140,000 people. Flint is predominantly black and predominantly poor. With over 40% of its
people living below the poverty line. Most cities employ a cop for
every couple hundred people. Flint employs one cop for every 800
people. It's consistently on the FBI's list of most dangerous cities in
the nation. There wasn't an abundance of opportunity.

My family was raised on welfare. We grew up standing in the
food lines where churches gave boxes of food to the poor on certain days of the week. It wasn't in me to ask for help. Although I
couldn't yet vote I considered myself a grown man. If I was grown
I had no place blaming anyone. I had to take responsibility for my
own situation or I could never change it. It was up to us to make
something happen. I would need much more than a $150 check
a week to take care of the people around me, which was my main
concern. I wasn't going to be those 50 year old men flipping burgers or those 50 year old men playing local shows for 10 people. I

couldn't be that anyway because in a few short years I had acquired a handful of misdemeanor crimes on my record. So I got into what most teenagers did, selling drugs. I was after the most money in the shortest amount of time. I just needed something to hold us over because you know I was going to blow up any day now.

6

Vendettas

In the neighborhood a quarter ounce of soft was $200. You could front it for $250 if they thought you were good for it. Since I was white they thought I was good for it. They just thought I was a custo who's family had money or a college kid who did the shit. I know this because they told me so. I didn't bother to set the record straight because I didn't care and it didn't matter. It was better if they thought of me as a harmless student. I could come through a few times a week and if I ever messed up it wouldn't take much to find me and to do something about it. I was fine with this. I found the biggest book I could, called *Hitchhikers Guide to the Galaxy*, which no doubt belonged to one of my roommates, Doni, who was into this type of shit. Anyway, it was a few inches thick and I opened it to the middle, placed a CD on the center of the page and traced the CD over and over with a razor cutting a circle in the center of a few hundred pages to make a compartment an inch or so thick inside the book. This is where I kept my stash. I carried it around in my backpack with a handful of notebooks and papers and pencils and things. Really playing into the student role. I was packin' 70 some odd cut and individually bagged dime rocks. Keep two or three in your pocket.

I didn't know everything there was to know but when it comes to doing wrong there is always someone around who is willing to teach you. These people aren't around to do you any good or to help you in anyway rather to get something for themselves. Aside from basic things like how to cut dope, cook it and scale it there were other lessons to be learned. Like the difference between character and reputation. About how a reputation can only manifest and spread through others. Although one is important, without people to perpetuate a reputation it ceases to exist. Character is something more valuable. Character is with you when no one else is. Even now as I write this I know it is with a bit of bias. As I grew older and more hardened I moved away from the fun stuff kids are supposed to do. They didn't make me feel strong or more honorable. I pushed the unimportant good memories out of my mind leaving only the bullshit that stood out. I believed those other memories didn't benefit or serve me in anyway. So I deleted them. These days it would take an exorcist to bring them out.

I would set up shop downtown, standing there all day and night "working." Downtown was a lot different back then. These days there is a camera on every corner. Old buildings have been demolished and new ones are being built. Back then we could access any vacant building we found. Closed hotels and buildings that are still inhabitable are used for student housing. Back then it wasn't such a safe bet. College kids commuted. These days private security hired by our Emergency Relief Manager patrol the blocks to discourage any potential criminal activity. Back then it wasn't uncommon to see the McDonalds drive through window robbed at knife point. The apartments where gun battles used to take place are now vacated and cleaned up with markets and coffee shops.

When I was coming up, it was desolate, a free for all. My spot was what we called the mazes. These cement "mazes" are the same ones we would later film in our video for the song, "Fat Around the Heart." Looks like something MC Escher would've come up with. Anyway, a lot of old homeless or young drug addicts and prostitutes or anything in between lived, ate and shat down here. We called it "The Jungle." These were my stomping grounds. Just a few blocks away from the venue and our practice space and on the same street we lived off of. It was easy to walk back to the space and sleep after being out all night. Then I could just wake up there for practice on the weekend.

I had gotten into violent situations throughout my neighborhood in the past, but this period took it to the next level. It was in the mazes and surrounding neighborhoods where I witnessed constant arguing that accelerated to stabbings, shootings, robbery and rapes. Down here it was anything goes. It didn't matter your age, race, creed or color. This was exciting and attractive to me because I had no idea how sad, bleak or hopeless it truly was. I hadn't gained that perspective yet. I was a kid. I watched women shoot heroin in their necks. Some whores shot it between their toes so their track marks weren't visible to prospecting Johns. I watched bums nod out while shitting on the ground and fall back in their own shit and wear it for days. I watched a pregnant woman fight a man over drugs, her legs covered in blood. I thought maybe she was going into labor. She pulled a weapon on him after a short scuffle. A kitchen knife she carried in her jeans. The man threw her down and she landed on the knife and it buried itself deep in her chest. She walked around with a knife sticking out of her chest like a comical Halloween costume. This was life and for some strange reason I was very happy to have it as a part of my identity.

It took me a while to settle in, get to know who's who, what's what and start making money. During this period I would be out for hours and nothing would happen. I toughed through it only taking a break to eat once a day. A good friend of mine named Daru lived a couple houses down from us. I went to school with this cat and we had similar lives. We spent a lot of years in the bus station eating 25 cent Little Debbie cakes as meals. He had a job and a wife and was trying to go legit and stay out of trouble. Since I got so much love for him I'll keep it at that. One of our friends named Sloan lived with him and Sloan was trying to get in the game. I had known him a few years and he had a piece of shit Lumina so we agreed we would work off the same bag. His cousins were smokers and came through consistently so it made sense. I would hold the shit and Sloan would cruise around town trying to make plays.

One time his shitty Lumina rolled by and he said he had an older guy who wanted a 50. I hopped in the car and we went to a house on the west side. When I walked in I saw an old teacher of mine. He knew I recognized him and paused before continuing on. He didn't even have a bullshit excuse these types usually have like "Oh, this isn't for me" or "I'm getting this for a friend." I made the dope sale to my former teacher without flinching and left before he had the chance to smoke it. I wouldn't see this guy again for a handful of years, when he gave me my GED test under the pressures of my mom and probation. I scored a 785 landing in the 99th percentile and threw the certificate in the trash because it didn't mean shit to me.

It wasn't but a few months before Sloan got hooked on the shit. I had known him for some years since we were young but at this point I didn't flinch. I really didn't care who you were. I would sell to anyone. So he became a custo. He was a functional fiend. Had a car and maintained a job, did a little bit of hustlin' but was a fiend nonetheless. I had a little bit of trust for him because he had been reliable in the past with consignment and with handling money. Or when he fucked up some money he could hit me back with his work check. When things slowed up in my usual spot, Sloan had an idea and I made a mistake. He said he had a play an hour or two north where the prices were much higher and we could off load everything. We had done this before so I made the bad call of trusting his idea and loaded him up and sent him north. He would sit up there until it was gone. But he couldn't control himself and disappeared. I would eventually hear through the grapevine he would catch a gun case up north and go to jail. It wasn't the first person I had lost to drugs and it wouldn't be the last. Since he was so far away I told myself I'd shoot him when he came back around. If he were to hang around town I couldn't have waited for it to get out that he had run off on me. I would've had to hunt him down there and then and provide everyone with an example ...... Cash up front only.

Around this same time my older brother Germ was robbing our house for what little possessions we did have. I was never close with him. He was usually in jail or wherever. On top of that he had a drug habit and I heard he had HIV. He would come in the middle of the night or when he knew no one was home and finesse little petty shit out of the house. He would take money from my girlfriends if he could find it. He's one of those bottom feeding losers who goes around ripping off anyone who lets him get close enough. That's what family is for. So I told myself I would shoot him next time I saw him and kept it moving. Retaliation right this second wouldn't get the bills paid so I had to stay focused. These were my mistakes I had to correct. In the meantime I would have to front something without having the money for the last one which doesn't look good, but fuck it my choices were few. These were lessons I had to learn. No one can betray you if you never give them the opportunity to do so.

After every long day it would get dark and the street lights would come on. If I were around the house I would go outside and sit under the street lights to read until it was time to shower which was a ritual in itself. We lived across the street from the road commission. They had a building with a nice lawn and all that. We waited until night time. Not because it was wrong but because we were proud. The news had just put several people from our neighborhood including an acquaintance named Zip on blast. Their report was about poor families that had no electricity or water in their homes with young children. This embarrassed us so we had a certain method to taking showers. When the sun went down their sprinkler system would kick on and water the lawn in short spurts. We waited on the porch in our underwear with bars of soap in hand. When they kicked on we went running toward them. Several young men on the front lawn of this business in our draws. Anyway, we scrubbed away with bars of soap before they instantly cut off and switched to a set of sprinklers on the other side of the lawn. At this point we sprinted and fell all over one another and wrestled in the fresh cut grass to the next hot spot where we continued to "shower." The watering system never seemed to water enough. We would always walk away with suds and unrinsed ears and things. We didn't know it then but what was coming from the sprinklers was lawn treatment chemicals. This group of small time crooks were just some kids trying to get by at home. This idea stuck with me forever. In the years to come I faced many kids with guns in the streets and had several enemies for one reason or another. Regardless of how things turned out I always knew they probably went home to the same shitty life I had or worse, every day.

I'm guilty of touching on these ideas redundantly in my work and speech. The truth is there isn't five minutes in a day that pass without these stories or images haunting my thoughts. Part of me feels that shining a spotlight on the negative and addressing the short-comings is more motivating than championing a blindly optimistic point of view. Once I was walking out of a diner and a car appeared to be out of control on the road. It did a wide turn into the parking lot of the diner and didn't appear to slow down as it drifted toward the building. I stopped and watched just outside the front door. When it got close enough I saw the driver by himself in the car passed out on the wheel. The car hopped the parking block and hit the front of the building ten or twelve feet from me. This is when I noticed the whole back window of the car had been shot several times. Some employees came outside. I looked on as they screamed at each other to call the cops. I walked closer to the car to see a man slumped over the steering wheel with blood all over him. The back of his head had been shot a few times and pieces of it were missing. After a few minutes, EMT's and police showed up. They declared him dead and attempted to pull the body from the car. As they wrestled him from his seat chunks of what appeared to be brain or skull covered in hair fell to the ground. The back of his head was blown off. I walked off and put my headphones back on and thought up a few lines about it.

"I seen him slumped over the steering wheel/ brains climbing from his mouth. Muscles protruding from his wounds/ like even they wanted out. But nobody gets out..."

This type of shit would go on all week. But we would always get back to the local on the weekend for shows. We would often front a new project or rotate members or call it a new name and have a new sound, etc. This summer we would meet another placement named Twerk. Yon heard about this guy who could play Slipknot's "PEOPLE = SHIT" on the drums and we were eager to go see his band play. A rock band that played shit like "Pour Some Sugar on Me" but the drummer was really good. Hit really hard and was big. A few years younger than us. This guy had his own kit, nicer than all our shit combined, and he drove. He liked heavy music so we asked him if he wanted to maybe try out for our band which sat somewhere between metal and hardcore at the time. He showed up and we had one question, "We heard you could play "PEOPLE = SHIT?"" He said, "Yeah." When he was done we had one more question. "Can you play that again?" We had found a drummer.

After the weekend was over it was back to work. Friends from school getting shot and well off suburban kids coming to the city only to be hooked on drugs and remain in the streets panhandling or selling ass for a fix. I was around drugs constantly but still never had any temptation. If they were unattractive as a child and a curse as a young teen, now as an older teen they just weren't worth the money. I wanted to be focused at all times. Sneek told me this was called straight edge so I called it that although I had been that before understanding what it was and would always be that so the label didn't matter. The only good I saw come from drugs was from selling them, which I've always seen as a victimless crime.

I had read around this time Sam Harris' *The End of Faith: Religion, Terror and the Future of Reason* where he says, "It is time we realized that crimes without victims are like debts without creditors. They do not even exist. Any person who lies awake at night worrying about the private pleasures of consenting adults has more than just too much time on his hands; he has some unjustifiable beliefs about the nature of right and wrong." Of course there are plenty of stories to go around about teenage drug use and overdose and homicide, but these are byproducts of other things. I'm talking about the consensual exchange between two able minded individuals, which was my current occupation whether I liked it or not. It felt like a graduation of sorts because I was no longer stealing from a bunch of people who had worked for things. In my eyes I was earning it myself and I was proud to be able to provide for those around me. We weren't sleeping on the street, we had a house. We didn't have to pass around the same winter jacket and take turns going outside one at a time, we had clothes. We weren't going out and stealing and robbing, we had a "job" and I took it seriously. This passage brings to mind an idea Nietzsche articulates perfectly when he explains that cowardice can often be masqueraded as morality. To paraphrase he explains that those who out of fear may refrain from doing the things they have the urge to do so that they may do "what is right" or consistent with a certain social construct or belief are not moral beings but cowardice beings who lack courage and bravery. Doing the right thing because you're scared of the consequences doesn't make you a good person. It makes you a scared person. I think it's a mix of courage and fear. Some people may look at lives like ours with envy that we had the courage to live as we wanted. Right or wrong. Some may say we were in fear and didn't have the courage to work and create a better situation for ourselves. You could say the same about the square who doesn't have the courage to live the life he dreams about because of the fear he adheres to. Be it inflicted by himself or his community or his spouse or his job or the world in general. Ah whatever. Being more brave is not the same as being less afraid.

This reminds me of a shitty teacher I had who spoke out against me in his classes regularly. He thought it was part of his job to tell his classes that I was a hypocrite because I sold drugs (this apparently was common knowledge) but I didn't do drugs. I learned this oddly enough while making transactions with students who were between classes. I had already dropped out, but this school was near downtown and I had gained business traction there. So a few times a week I would walk over to the lot bordering the school yard and hand things through the fence to the students who had accumulated. This was so if any teacher, security or school police tried to get at me I was already on the other side of a nine foot tall fence giving me a solid advantage on escaping. I would have a long line of a couple dozen students formed along the fence. It's funny to imagine this scenario like a free man on the other side of the prison yard gate. Selling contraband to those who are still imprisoned not physically but indoctrinated and confined mentally. Not that I believed I was free to be fair there was also a fence around my world and so on and so forth. Turtles all the way down. Anyway it was during these social encounters I would learn about the latest high school politics, i.e. this particular classroom announcement. To this day I don't really understand the hypocrisy but it's funny now to recall the slight. Even funnier that eventually the teacher would go on to have a sexual relationship with one of his students whom which I had already played, so I got the last laugh. That being said most teachers continued to resemble my peers more closely than any kind of role model. Half of them were on drugs. I reminded myself that even the most prestigious psychiatrists often see psychiatrists and participate in the prescription drug industry themselves. This didn't mean I didn't agree with it, it meant I couldn't.

Anyway, I spent whole nights walking the area through. Junkies and prostitutes became the people I spent most of my time around. It served as a lesson in social dynamics. When we worked at the shows at the venue you turned this off. You couldn't treat concert goers like you treated some fiend on the street. You learn to separate the different areas of your life and keep them from overlapping. I tried to isolate each half of my life from the other and keep those on one side ignorant that the other side existed. I had been doing this my whole life anyway with all my caretakers. When it came to females I tried keeping them ignorant to as much of both sides as I could. In some minimal ways it's okay to let pieces share the same place and time. For example, when I was working in the street I would use it as an opportunity to write and rehearse songs in my head. Reciting freestyle pieces or concocting poems or passages until they were memorized. At this point I had discovered and read a lot about long-term memory. The ability to commit long passages or large lists of items to memory by associating cues. World Memory Champions believed the brain and memory can be exercised into development like a muscle. Some could memorize 54 packs of playing cards, over 2800 cards in total, after looking at them once. I had also read and studied the life of the Notorious BIG and Jay-Z and Lil Wayne whom I considered a great. These three also didn't write their songs down because of the same dilemmas. If they could do it I could do it. I started writing in my head. After successfully crafting several songs this way I would never write another one down. I would work to sharpen this spoken word stream of consciousness ability over the next ten plus years.

Between Twerk's car and Sneek's girlfriend's car we could now travel to play shows out of town. Until then we had been playing the same venue for over a year, now we could expand. We would fill Twerk's car with his drums and he would ride alone. We would fill Sneek's girl's trunk with gear and all ride with her and one of our friends usually had a car that a dozen other people piled into to the go the show and not pay to get in of course. We could travel to Lansing or some country town to play in makeshift venues that more resembled barns and houses. These places packed in about 30-50 people into them and we didn't get paid. Sometimes we would get lucky in the Detroit area and play an actual venue with a stage and sound system but when that happened no one knew who we were and no one came and we didn't get paid there either. Everyone has this same story. After the shows on the weekends it was time to focus on work.

It didn't take long for people to recognize what I was doing in the neighborhood. I was the only white boy with red hair in the area with this particular occupation. Being from a predominantly black city meant the majority of those working around me were black. My skin color was both a blessing and a curse. The police didn't give me too hard of a time because I didn't fit into the usual pro-file. Some hustlers as I said thought I was a college kid because of the backpack or they didn't bother with the analyzation at all and considered me soft. Some folks just thought I was a cop and stayed away from me. Which I was fine with unless you were a customer. I had to cut stones bigger than the next guy to attract customers. If it wasn't bigger stones I had to offer more pieces for the same price to get them gone. This was just how it went. It didn't offend me and I didn't think anything of it. I was the minority and that's how minorities are treated. If I were the only black guy working a white block it would've been the same thing. I began to see where that school of thought came from but I wouldn't be affected by it. Some people would be receptive, some are indifferent and some wouldn't tolerate it. I didn't want a reputation. I didn't want to be anybody, I just wanted money. Sometimes it would occur to me I was tak-ing money out of someone else's pocket or food out of someone else's mouth but I really didn't care. I didn't care about myself how could I care about somebody I didn't know. My attitude was 'do something.' The opportunity to prove myself in any situation was something I waited for. Many times, many individuals did decide to 'do somethin.' Once I was listening to music when I got snuck up on from behind by three kids with one gun. A stick up. I had no gun and was outnumbered so I just gave it up. They told me to throw it on the ground in front of me and turn around. Probably a couple hundred dollars cash. I now kept the drugs in my shoes and lost the backpack. Whenever I was making a sale I only appeared to have 2-3 rocks which I kept in my pocket. So I wasn't completely put out but it was another lesson learned. I didn't tell anyone about it because I didn't want word to get around that I was a target. I also didn't ask anyone for help for the same reason. Instead I thought about how I would get even. I could afford to catch up with Sloan or my brother whenever was convenient but this was something I would have to go after. I had to choose where, when and how to fight this battle.

7

Revenge

I sat around for a few days reading book after book. Sun Tzu's *The Art of War* and *48 Laws of Power* by Robert Greene. Thinking about what to do and asking around town for a gun. While I deliberated I got a call from my mom out of the blue. (You didn't have to have electricity to have a landline plugged into the phone jack). I hadn't seen her since she moved out. Her and my aunt wanted to take all of us kids to a rollercoaster park in Sandusky Ohio a few hours outside of Flint. I had been there once before but it wasn't a place we frequented. I was confused. Then she told me she was planning to move to Florida. She had ten brothers and sisters living down there, save for my one uncle who was chipping away at some decades in prison here in Michigan, and she saw it as a chance at a better life. She needed a change. She wanted to do this one last trip before we all moved down south. She thought I would follow her down there. It made sense because she was taking my family away. I hadn't seen my dad in some years.

I wasn't leaving Flint for anything. I had no job, no way of living and no guaranteed future but I wasn't going anywhere. I could've given up and started over elsewhere. Away from the disgusting house with no water or electricity. Away from the stick up kids who were still in the street waiting for my return. Away from hustling to survive. Away from the bed with maggots in it. But I couldn't quit. I would be giving up. I was focused and I felt as if the core of my being was infused with my city. I told her we would go to the park but I wouldn't be moving anywhere. She said her and her sister would be over in two days early morning and to have my things packed. She thought I would come around. Little did she know in the next 2 days the child she was talking to on the phone would be dead and gone. She would have an entirely different person for a son.

The next night me and a guy I knew from the street, we can call him Shortie, were making our way back to my place around 3-4 AM and I was tired. I had been out all night. We were both out of drugs. Shortie was even out of the dummy rocks he had made up. Completely out. I kept long nails in those days to break stones. When I ran out of bagged stuff I would scrape under my nails for the residue that would build up underneath. Then I'd push it together with my fingers to forge a rock. Not banana yellow but speckled black from all the dirt that I also scraped and mixed in there. The customers never noticed. Sometimes daily activities trigger these memories. Like when you rip open a head of lettuce and smell the inside. That's what crack smells like. Or at least that's what my shit smelled like. For all you squares who are reading this as entertained as you can be. Even some brands of Chapstick like Burt's Bees take me on a trip. Anyway I had the stick up in the back of my mind and was plotting revenge but continued working until the solution revealed itself. Shortie asked to use our home phone to have someone come and pick him up. I said okay but I was anxious for him to leave because my mom would be there in just a few hours to take me and my friends to the rollercoaster park. Now that I think of it, I don't know if Shortie even had a house. He wasn't really my boy, he definitely wasn't crew, he was just a guy from the same neighborhood. An acquaintance. Anyway, his phone convo sounded like he owed this person money but it wasn't my business and I really didn't care. My thoughts were elsewhere.

I sat on the porch while Shortie waited for his ride to see him off. A car with tints pulled up into the driveway. Shortie leaned in on the driver side and started talking. After a brief back and forth I saw a gun come out the window, a revolver, shot four or five times. Shortie jerked and jumped and fell to the ground. This didn't faze me. I continued sitting on the porch. I knew this person, his name was Bama. I knew he didn't have a problem with me. I stood up as the car pulled off. Shortie was screaming and kicking around on the ground. I calmly walked over to him. Where his shorts left his legs bare bullets had visibly buried themselves. Higher up his legs more wounds leaked visible streams of blood down his body and onto the ground. I asked him if he wanted me to call an ambulance or get Domonic. Domonic was the next door neighbor and Shortie's friend who had an ol' lady, both of which worked and had kids and were sleeping which is why he didn't use their phone. He said to call an ambulance so I walked inside as he screamed and crawled toward Domonic's porch. I told all my roommates what had happened. My girlfriend at the time was tripping out like girls do. I picked up the phone, our only luxury, and said someone had been shot and hung up. The police would show up and cuff us all immediately. We were sat on the curb and questioned. Does anyone have a weapon on them? No. Whose house is this? Ours. Do you mind if we search it? Of course not (I was out of drugs). Are there weapons in the house? No. Did anyone see what happened? No. Does anyone know the shooter? No. Did anyone get a look at the car? No. How do you know the victim? I don't. Shortie would be taken away in an ambulance and he wouldn't say a word either. The cops pulled off at about 7-8 AM just as a van was pulling up to load up and go to the rollercoaster park. It was going to be a long day.

The day at the park is kind of a blur. We rode down like I imagine a typical family does. My mom, my aunt, me and Don, plus about a dozen friends and cousins and siblings piled into a minivan. We were questioned about what the cops were doing at the house when they pulled up. I tried to hide as much as I could from my mom but since she had seen and done it all there wasn't too much that would shock her if it ever came out. I imagine her reading this book and laughing quite a bit. We explained what happened almost in a proud way. After the couple hour drive we parked and made our way towards the gates while my aunt divided up the tickets. Once inside, we proceeded as any group of teenagers would proceed segregating ourselves from the smaller kids and the adults so we could roam free and terrorize anyone in the park we came into contact with. The place is fun. You stand in line for 1-2 hours waiting to get on a rollercoaster that takes you around a track for 1-2 minutes. In the lines we would try to talk to girls or make fun of other people or ourselves. On the rides we screamed obnoxious stupid shit that made no sense and probably offended everyone within earshot. It's one of those places where you forget about the life you have to go back to. For 8-10 hours we ran around from ride to ride. Only stopping for a hotdog or an elephant ear or when we ran into other people from our group. The day quickly passed and it was time to go back home which I was anxious for. Even during enjoyable times my mind was on how I could be progressing toward my goals and that having an enjoyable time was not progress. We piled back into the van and rode home. My mom talked about moving and about how serious she was. She condemned the city as I had heard so many before her do. Blaming it for every problem she had or saying that it lacked just this one thing that was contingent on her having a good life. I told her I wasn't moving. She kept reminding me to think about it like I hadn't already as she pulled back into Flint to drop us off at home.

As we pulled up in front of our house I saw Bama playing in Dom's lawn with his little kids. Dom didn't seem very comfortable with his presence but was the weaker of the two so had to play along. I knew what time it was. As the van pulled away Bama walked over and I let my boys know to go inside. He motioned for me to start walking with him. He asked what I saw last night and I said "nothin." He asked me what I told the police and I said "nothin." Seeing and saying nothing is a good response if you want to keep your life. I said as little as possible and walked as casual as I could. I knew he had a gun. He was a lot bigger than me. He asked me if I had a gun and I told him no. He asked me if I had a car and I said no. I was so tired at this point and I was thinking about my current situation. If this dude reaches for his gun do I fight him or try and shove him over and get behind something he saw my aunt's car he knows theres more people at the house. That kind of confusion. It seemed like he was making shit up as he went along. Like he hadn't thought exactly about his next move. He said I would have to prove it to him, prove I was real, prove I was solid. He needed something to hang over my head so he asked if I had beef with anyone. Through my daydreaming the three stick up kids popped into my mind. That night would be the beginning of a close friendship. "I'll drive, you shoot." he said. I realized I hadn't slept in a couple days but I knew I had no choice. I recall being a bit delirious and going in and out like a dream. As Ray Bradbury put it, "There was a sound of thunder."

I chilled out at home for a while reading a lot of books. Laying low. I had now picked up from a couple books a month to three books a week. We stole them from the Borders or the used bookstores around town. The ones that we couldn't find in stores we would sit at the library and read or steal. Back then you could check out a dozen books at a time. One of my favorite books is still Seneca the Youngers "On the Shortness of Life." The book clicks on so many different levels I wouldn't know where to begin. Amongst the hundreds of masterful passages I recall taking away two main points that are driven home throughout the work. The first one summed up in a passage that reads: "We are in the habit of saying that it is not in our power to choose the parents who are allotted to us, that they were given to us by chance. But we can choose whose children we would like to be." You can find them in others or in books and stories they have written. They can be dead wise men from the past. Seneca also made me feel okay about being poor or helped me to understand the nature of poverty. Understanding that money is of no value and time is a precious resource when he writes: "You will find no one willing to share out his money; but to how many does each of us divide up his life! People are frugal in guarding their personal property; but as soon as it comes to squandering their time they are most wasteful of the one thing in which it is right to be stingy." This is something everyone knows. Its parroted everywhere and packaged and sold countless times over but as with most pieces of wisdom the mouth speaks it tirelessly but the body betrays it endlessly. I didn't just read the words I understood them and they would alter my path.

Reading was never uncool to me. If you were a free man and you read a lot, you were a nerd but I have a handful of friends, people I looked up to, who were much older serving decades in prison and were some of the smartest people I talked to. These were inspiring people to me. When you read 150 books a year, mostly nonfiction, you start to connect a bunch of dots. Your awareness and your consciousness expands. I would read something then read every book in the bibliography, and so on. You start building a solid web of knowledge or a sense of connectedness. You also become aware of how fragmented the general way of thinking and doing things is. Anyway, this was around the time I was trying to understand Quantum Physics books by Bohr and Bohm, which didn't work the first read but through the years I would be able to comprehend about 1% of them. I would find identifiable real life characters in books. I didn't find it unusual to carry guns and be involved in shootouts and other things I shouldn't had been doing. All of this didn't feel wrong because when I came home early in the morning with a pocket full of money I would count through the change and the 1's and 5's and 10's and the occasional 20 dollar bill. I would look at the 20 and recall stories I had read of Andrew Jackson, the man who ran the country from 1829-1837. This is a man riddled with bullets, who was said to have clanked when he walked, not from war but from multiple duels in the street. Soon enough I would find out what it was like to be riddled with bullets as well.

In the circles I associated with there was honor in mutual combat. There was of course no honor in preying upon women children or squares but violence wasn't a stigmatized ignorant alternative to intelligent action. Of course that's the way it's being painted today. It isn't my interest to justify or endorse violence, it never has been. I only wish to illustrate that my idols, who all can agree were great men, always stood for what they believed in and met adversity head on and so forth.

Sociology and psychology were topics of interest to me. I thought they explained the world around me. I appreciated the work of Italian socialist Corrado Gini who came up with the Gini index which was a very simple scale of 0 and 1 that measured the distribution of wealth in a region. Defining the haves and have nots. Plenty others would go on to confirm that the astoundingly high correlation between poverty and violence or wealth and violence wasn't so cut and dry but that relative poverty is what produced violent results amongst young men. Places with absolute wealth as we know usually fair alright. Also places like areas of India where absolute poverty exists aren't necessarily known for their violence. Its places where affluence and poverty live within reach of one another that breeds violence. This seemed to make sense and would lead me to the work of psychologists Margo Wilson and Martin Daly originally because I was attracted to their book called *Homicide* and the chalk outline on the cover. They were immersive journalists which I appreciated a bit more than the dilettante who reads three search engine headlines, quickly formulates a shallow opinion, and proceeds to broadcasts it on the internet under the guise of journalism. Following this work through the years Daly explained that it is logical and even necessary for young men in these kinds of environments to commit violent acts. I'm paraphrasing here but the idea in a nutshell is that the violent act makes complete sense when one lacks a career or education or long life expectancy. When one does not participate in the typical westernized rat race he must jock for position in his own world another way. So he reverts back to aggression because there are no other means in sight. Daly did some studies in Detroit and found only half the solved cases go to court for 2nd degree murder. If they do go to court no one will testify or it will most likely be considered mutual combat. From there most of the time they will not go in front of a jury but will plea bargain the 2nd degree to manslaughter. After being sentenced to a few years and getting out after 18 months you emerge from prison with the same assets you went in with plus some. You now are more revered. You have a more fearsome reputation in the street and you have advanced and upped your status socially from killing. This is more valuable than a house or a car in a lot of ways so in these types of situations it is one of few logical options to take. This is not how it should be but how it is.

Anyway after awhile I was starting to make a decent amount of money hustling. You remember the ceilings you break hustlin'. The first time you make a thousand dollars or ten thousand etc. I was working toward the ten thousand dollar ceiling. Far from rich but making better than a minimum wage check. I spent it all on food and equipment for the crew. We started accumulating some decent gear. This made it more appealing to practice and get better as a group. I didn't spend any of the money paying the bills. I saw that as a lost cause. The bills were thousands of dollars past due and I thought shoveling us out of that hole would take away from our music, which was the top priority.

The neighborhood was getting hot. Police were everywhere suddenly. Shortie had gotten shot and was still in the hospital. He would live. On the next block over a kid had knocked on an older man's door and shot him dead over an argument. Most recently our house had been in the middle of a gun fight with police and Zip. This put everyone on high alert. The police presence was just something that came with it the way I saw it. I was raised as a kid to hate police as an enemy. Like most kids around me I had plenty reason. They would do foul shit like make you lift your dick and spread your ass then make you put your hands in your mouth to look under your tongue. This was unnecessary at best but through my life I would witness it to the extreme. I saw them beat a few of my friends unnecessarily. I've had them lie in their paperwork and steal money and drugs from me and people I knew. They often took the people I love away to prison who knows how many times. In jail I saw them handcuff men to the bench then proceed to beat them unconscious or tase them until they threw up all over themselves. I also have experienced the extreme of knowing men who have been shot to death by police. I feel like these experiences give me some authority to touch on the subject. I will just say that a handful of them make it easy to hate them all but over the years I would come to an understanding that being a policeman was just a job. This probably had something to do with discovering authoritarianism and stumbling across the Stanford Prison Experiment by Phil Zimbardo or reading through the Abu Ghraib scandal. The uniform doesn't make a good man bad or bad man good. The uniform can make a weak man bad but it can also augment the capabilities of a man with good character. To be clear, under no circumstances would I call for their assistance. But I think the police are a good thing for women and children and squares to call upon. That's their purpose. Over the years I met a few that were solid men and women. They came up in the same neighborhoods that we were all raised in, knew some of the same people and had nothing in common with the typical boogeyman with a badge and a gun. So from here on out I just looked at it as they had a job to do and so did I, to stay clear of them. We happen to be on opposite teams but common sense told me not make more enemies than I already had. Plus you couldn't fight this gang. So I tried to treat everyone with respect and not make any unnecessary enemies. This is not as black and white as most put it however this is not the popular opinion mainstream media pushed so we can overlook it.

As the winter approached we prepared to move houses. We had been evicted and anyone living the lifestyle knows it takes a couple of months to get someone out of a house. We planned on moving down town

Soon afterward my mom would move down south like she had planned. She took my brothers and sisters and I stayed in Flint with the crew. I kept in touch with her a couple times a year. If I did need something now she wasn't around to even entertain the idea. No one was and that didn't bother me. So without a conclusion, without a lesson or a summary or some surprise ending, the story continues with the same kind of bullshit with which it began.

8

Midwest Monsters

After getting thrown out of our last house we would kick around town like a nomadic group. We used anyone's name who still had credit and hadn't yet been burned by the debt of bills and evictions over the years. This worked to get us into a place and get the utilities turned on but with no money we could only ride out a few months before getting evicted again. I was hustlin' but wasn't making any kind of money to pull real weight. A lot of the guys were jackin' too. Anyone in the area around this time knows we were infamous for jackin' whatever may have some value to it. We kept the things we liked and sold what we didn't and used the money for food but jackin' isn't a real hustle especially in a place where nobody has shit. We stored our gear wherever we could while we walked around town all day trying to keep ourselves distracted. When we had no house we could always go to the library during the day and continue to sit and read or write and talk. When the library closed we would resort to the diners. The diners we hadn't recently done an eat and run at anyway. We could all pile into the diners and split a dollar cup of coffee and sit there for hours out of the cold passing the cup around until our appetite was suppressed and our bodies thought we were full.

We got to know the waitresses and the owners of the diners. A lot of kids hung out in the diners to have coffee and smoke cigarettes and talk about stupid shit like politics. A lot of nights we had nowhere else to go. It wasn't uncommon to sit inside at a table for 12 hours or more before moving to the next one. There was a 24 hour spot near downtown that we could camp out in. I remember a few days we sat there the whole day. Breakfast lunch and dinner time and when it got dark I would continue sitting through the night. Some of my friends didn't have as much patience branching off here and there to find something to do but some days I recall sitting there drinking several pots of coffee while reading one book after another. We did this for years and I still find myself sitting in these places drinking pots of coffee staring at people. Today it's something I enjoy. Back then it was just what we had to do. I think this made us stronger people. It thickened our skin. Going days without showering or changing clothes. Sleeping outside gives you an appreciation that can't be taught. This would be the state of affairs for the next couple years, back and forth between homeless and temporary living spots. Not showering until it didn't bother you anymore. Sleeping outside in the cold until it didn't bother you anymore. Not eating until it didn't bother you anymore. Being disappointed until you didn't let it happen anymore.

In one of these houses, I watched Gar die. Or at least I thought so. I'll only say that recently he had been in a near fatal house explosion that left him hospitalized and in a coma for a while. After, he was given a morphine drip for pain and released with a strong pain-killer prescription. Gar was lying on the couch taking handfuls of pills. I paid it no mind as it wasn't an unusual sight. I assumed his tolerance was high. A few minutes passed before Yon yelled from the next room that he thought Gar was dead. He was motionless and didn't appear to be breathing. Yon leaned over his body and started taking things like money, prescription pills and anything else of value, robbing this presumably dead body. I ran over and felt his chest to find a heartbeat. There was a faint beat every few seconds, or what seemed like it. The pulse was sparse. I realized there was no car around, no house phone or cell phone either. The closest resource I could think of was the diner two or three blocks away. He surely had a car. I threw Gar over my shoulder and ran up a few blocks into the diner. He was wrapped in bandages he was required to change daily that were undoubtedly weeks old. He was heavy and smelled like shit and bled everywhere from the rough treatment to his freshly wounded skin or whatever it was. I walked through the door with him and asked a waitress I knew to get somebody. This place was used to these types of things. The owner came out from the back room and quickly agreed to run us to the hospital. We got out front to his pickup truck, some kind of old Chevy. When I went to put him inside he told me to throw him in the bed of the truck, then mumbled something in his foreign language about, "drugs." I threw Gar in the bed of the truck and hopped up front and we made our way to Hurley hospital nearby. I walked in and dropped Gar at emergency and they rushed him to the back. I left before anyone could come and question me. They said his heart stopped but they revived him. He would sit in the hospital a little longer before being released again. Taking into account the hell my dawg would inflict on the city in the years to come I imagine many people are upset I didn't let him die but I like to think this act went toward my karmic debt.

This house was our current practice space. It was the same crew but we had recently added a couple guitar players named Beal and Rick. Beal was a young tattooed party animal that Twerk had met. He brought him around and since he was pretty good and liked the blues we started playing together. Rick was a long haired metal head that wanted to play death metal. I just went with it because the novelty was good enough. Plus I wasn't doing anything else. We were playing real fast music at this time and we were evolving as a band. I wasn't ecstatic about death metal but as long as I could keep writing and working out songs that was what was important. Yon dropped out because he didn't like the direction. Sneek dropped out to play with another group and Gene moved to bass. I'm not too embarrassed about the writing I was putting out at this time or at least what it could potentially become. Although we were homeless every couple months we had collected nice gear so that was no longer an issue. We were playing around the state more and getting known a bit.

We had to leave that house when the landlord set it on fire while we were still inside. We believe for insurance money. The fire was started in the basement and we were on the second floor. This was one of those quadruplexes, a large house split into four separate units. When smoke started pouring through the vents we left all of our things and grabbed our music gear and hauled it outside on to the front lawn. The man who owned the local venue lived across the street. He was friendly with us and offered to let us store our equipment at his place while we figured out where we were going. We appreciated this gesture. We had stopped playing this venue a few years prior because it had shut down for remodeling. It would end up staying closed for several years but we would cross paths with all the old staff and friends around town over the years. Today I think these guys believe I'm painting Flint in a violent light. I understand this. Still, I believe acknowledging the flaws, being honest about the negative and addressing the issues are important if you want to get things get solved. I also think our experiences of the city vary drastically. All that aside these guys don't get stopped by TSA every time they fly due to the bullet fragments and shrapnel buried in their bodies. But we'll get to that.

We would kick around from house to house over the next couple years focusing on reading and writing and music. Every now and then I would get the hunch to go back and try my hand at school or trying to work a legitimate job. Both of these quickly fell by the way side after a couple weeks. I would rather be homeless and hungry. I would pick up a couple hobbies, like weight training. I was getting a mental workout on a day to day basis but that was only half the battle so I started seeking physical tests as well. Besides, being in better shape would give me a physical advantage over the next person. Most people want to look good for girls. I wanted to bust heads. I was known as a fighter. I had been in hundreds of fights up to this point and it wasn't unusual to fight 3-4 times a week for years on end. Comin' up it was either because of the way I looked or because I was a white boy who liked black girls in a black city. I don't know how many times I fought dudes over that tired idea. As I got older most of the fights I was involved in I was just sticking up for my shitty friends. Either way I would fight anybody anywhere over anything they wished to quarrel over. I would fight five people by myself if that's what came up.

It's in me to fight. My bloodline is from Scotland. The northern tip of the highlands right near the Orkney Islands. My family belongs to the Gunn Clan, whose motto is "Aut Pax Aut Bellum." Either Peace or War. Seemed fitting enough to me. I wasn't big on starting fights, I wasn't the loudest person in the room and I didn't believe in picking on people. Usually I was defending myself or one of my friends who was most likely in the wrong. The shitty part about fighting these days is it doesn't matter who starts the quarrel. The person lying there bleeding when all is said and done is now the poor victim and the person who "wins" is looked at as a bully type. Not that I always won. I had my head laid open by pistols, my skin parted by knives, my ribs broken with bats, hit by cars, my skull cracked with rocks, all my fingers and toes, both hands and feet broken several times and got hundreds of stitches to name a few incidents from fighting alone. But winning or losing didn't matter. After a while I didn't get in my feelings or become out of control. I just liked to fight. This gave our large group a good reputation in the streets but a bad reputation around the real world which included the music scene. We had been making poor choices around town for as long as we could remember but nothing that affected our music life. This slowly changed over the years when physical altercations came up. We considered ourselves family. When one fought we all fought. That's how it went. We just weren't okay with letting someone hurt one of us. Yes it's cowardly if you are scared to fight another man one on one and have to rely on your friends but we weren't scared of anyone we simply didn't respect anyone enough to give it any thought. We were a pack of animals that didn't concern themselves with the logic of man.

Around this same time I got into MMA fighting, specifically Muay Thai and Brazilian Jiu Jitsu. I exclusively read books about fighting. Beliefs, techniques, origins whatever it may be. You didn't need money or an education for this kind of hobby so I was in to practice it hours a day.

This same summer I got it in my mind that the military might be a good path for me. Being a soldier peeked my interest for many reasons. I already had an affinity for firearms and combat. You needed no degree and I didn't yet have any felony convictions on my record yet nor did I tattoo my hands. I considered this was a part of my path. I became close with a kid I'll call Sid. He was just graduating and looking at military prospects. So I did too. I had a real love for this kid and would go to the end of the earth for him much like a lot of my friends. What drew me in aside from being paid to fight was the accountability. Every man was responsible for pulling his own weight. The terms were very cut and dry. I never for a second thought that I would not train as hard as possible, get in, go to war, fight hard and come home with enough money to continue my musical pursuits. I didn't agree with the current politics of that time but I didn't care. I wanted to be a soldier and politics weren't on my mind. I wanted to be dropped somewhere to see how I would fair. I wanted to be tested.

When I read the journals from this year it's very schizophrenic and scatter brained. I'm trying to come up with a new life plan or way out every day it seems. If this seems all over the place it's because I was. It wasn't that I wasn't focused but I wasn't getting results so I stayed focused on the things I wanted to pursue and continued to try absolutely anything I heard about. Most often I would run into harsh realizations or dead ends but I was at rock bottom and since I had no one to answer to I had a lot of time on my hands.

Anyway we trained for the better part of a year together. Physical training with Sid was tough because it wasn't about strength. We swam a few miles, hopped out, did as many push-ups pull ups and sit ups as you could then running a few miles then doing it all over again. He was in much better shape than I was. We would think up routines that we considered impossible for us and then attempt them. We would run the standard PST daily to improve our times which were already passing. When that became boring we would run it with weighted vests and so on. I worked this into my studies and became familiar with weapons systems from some of the first made up to the more modern technologies. Learned about war and legendary soldiers from the past. Learned about battle formations and protocols. I wanted to be as ready as a person could be. I cheated off Sid on our ASVAB test so they thought I was a genius. Soon after we received a ship out date or Sid did rather. I had a hang up about my criminal record. I was on probation in Florida and Michigan for assaulting dudes but was re assured it was minor and could be remedied. So I would work on getting it squared away and follow right behind Sid after he left. This never happened. Shortly after this I would witness another murder. My cousin was killed by his brother in law and everyone present was taken into custody for being there when the cops showed up. After our stories made it clear we weren't involved we were released. Over the following months I was subpoenaed to give deposition after deposition over the next couple months which held me up from my military plans which I felt slipping from my grasp. The brother in law got away with it though if that says anything. I would be incarcerated shortly after this and that would hold me up even longer. Dead end.

While all of this was going on we were living in a house downtown, not far from the one that was set on fire a year prior. There were three connected brick units. We lived in one unit. The area was drug infested. I sold a few college books that I was reading and opened up shop undercutting everyone in the neighborhood. My plan was to keep the ship afloat while I tried jumping through all the hoops to ship out. I would make the most of it because I didn't know if it would be a week or a year. Over the following months our shop grew. We hustled all day and all night and played music right in the living room of the house while we were working. We went over time and sold everything. Weed was $600 a pound and went for $100 an ounce. A jar of XTC (500 pills) was $250 and would go for $15-20 a pill. Coke was $700 an ounce and would go for $75 a gram. Acid. Mushrooms. Pills. Heroin. We would make a few grand on a good day. Sometimes on the first of the month we would have a line going out of the house around back and to the street. There were loud parties, a hundred people littered on the front lawn. We fought right in the yard, we shot guns in the street for fun whether it was day or night or at another person or in the air. The neighbors called the cops on us and when they came we sacked up all our shit and ran and hid out at a homegirls house. Then we'd sit at the park nearby weighin' shit and bustin' sales right out in the open until the coast was clear to return to the house. The squares in the neighborhood hated our guts. The hustlers in the neighborhood did too because a bunch of "college boys" took all their business. This meant we had to stand our ground or be bullied out of business. When we were threatened we would brawl or shoot it out in the street. When dudes sicced their dog on me I would pull the SKS from under the porch, middle of the day, right there in the front lawn. When cats threatened to kill us I would chase them through the neighborhood shooting at them. These things were exciting and they came with the territory but it wasn't at the top of our list. The only things we really wanted to be doing were sleeping with more girls than we could count and making more money than we could count. I remember riding around in a stolen convertible with two hoes in the front and a jar of ecstasy. Hanging out the back was me and my cousin shooting stop signs for no reason. We were some dumb ass hustlers. We would work with anyone right on the spot. Someone would want something and only have $3. We didn't know what that shit even looked like so we broke them off something small. Someone would have $9 or $14 and we just worked with whatever they had. Whatever needed to be done. This is the environment KING was conceived in.

KING was me Gene, Twerk, Beal and San. Rick had left and San took his place. We met him shortly after we moved in. He had moved up to Flint from Texas to play in another band that was signed. I assume he moved on this street because it was cheap housing but we landed right next door to him. He liked heavy music and we would hear it coming out of his window from our porch. Over time we started playing and he was good. Eight of us lived in one unit. Beal and Twerk moved into the second unit with another one of our friends and San would move into the 3rd unit with even more of our friends. He wanted to start something with us in addition to his other band. Something heavier. He didn't spend his days the same way we did but for the music we were down. We started KING in December 2007 in that compound full of friends. In January 2008 my unit was raided and six of us were arrested. Even my girlfriend was handcuffed and questioned. She stayed solid and didn't say anything more than she had to. I still owe her for that one. When they took me away I knew she wouldn't be around when I get out regardless of when that was. That was what we called "this life no one wants."

Sitting by myself in that cell was one of the best things that ever happened to me. I sat alone thinking for days. Doing thousands of pushups and sitting silent in a meditative state. I recalled stories about Seneca and Socrates and Boethius who all philosophized while imprisoned and awaiting execution. I didn't know how long I would be in there. The police had discovered and seized drugs, handguns and money. I thought about my own life and where I was headed. I thought we were damned. Growing up how we grew up. I thought this jail thing was all a part of the life we chose and that I better accept it. I thought it was difficult to go to the military before and now it must be impossible. I started to write passages in my head. About our lives. I could recall the instrumental the guys were working on that day. I went to working on it. Thinking up lines. I had no paper or pencil. I didn't even have a blanket or pillow. I was working with myself. I memorized line after line just like I had on the street so many years before. I crafted and committed each chunk of sentences to memory. Since I had nothing but time I added mathematical themes throughout the passage like I had heard of TOOL doing. The song was appropriately about violence and jail and the world around us. I built double and triple entendres in the lines. I riddled the text with numerical values. I worked hours committing each nuance to permanent memory.

This is where my head was at. I wrote our first song in solitary confinement at the Genesee County Jail. And so RICO was born.

R.I.C.O

5 Lock and load. 1

4 Duck down, when you hear the sound of one hundred rounds tear your house to the ground.

3 That's how they're getting down downtown.

2 We're killing over color and we're heaven sent and hell bound.

1 Father wasn't around to beat me down.

16 I'm a conscious less psychopath on the streets of a ghost town.

15 Bodies slumped on their steering wheels, brains climbing from their mouths, muscles protruding from their wounds, like even they want out. 2

14 Nobody gets out. 3

13 Nobody ever makes it out and before I drew my head from the cunts mouth...

12 One foot was in the grave. 4

11 We're dying so young where I come from.

10 It's gun or be gunned.

9 Run or be ran over man over man.

8 Foolhardy as they come.

7 As kids we skipped the fun.

6 Fascinated with numbers and ways we could make them run.

5 Fascinated with numbers and ways we could make them run.

4 Unaware we had just hung the possibility of a kosher become. 5
3 It's so damn dark, out here ◆hailstones blot out the sun.

2 Bodies, buried atop one and other. 6
1 Cutters, keep on hacking up my brothers.
8 Bodies, buried atop one and other.
7 Cutters, keep on hacking up my brothers.

6 They're letting shots loose from Sacramento to ♠Syracuse. 7
5 I dreamt I put it all behind me then I awoke too...

4 Sounds of busting guns. 8
3 Bullet holes in lungs.
2 Taste your guts sliding off of your tongue.
1 Tendons bone fragments lodged in your gum's.
4 Mothers praying for the health of their sons.

3 Sickens me, what we've become. 9
2 Sickens me, what we've become.

1 Bodies, buried atop one and other. 10
2 Cutters, keep on hacking up my brothers.
1 Bodies, buried atop one and other.
1 Cutters, keep on hacking up my brothers.

♠ Syracuse problem, also known as Collatz conjecture after Lothar Collatz is
an unsolvable mathematical conjecture, 3n + 1.
If a number is odd triple it and add one.
If the number is even divide it in half.
Any number eventually gets to 0.

♦ Reference to the Hailstone sequence or hailstone numbers which is a reference to the number sequence and how they fall.

one - There are six mentions of this number in the song which serves as the first number entered into the equation which pans out; 6,3,10,5,16,8,4,2,1

3 - The next number in the sequence. There are three perspectives or points of view in this song. Although the content is consistent there are two major movements. The first POV is from a more involved and aggressive demeanor. This POV morphs with the lines "Nobody gets out. Nobody ever makes it out." into a more pitiful and sympathetic perspective. With the lines "They're letting shots loose from Sacramento to Syracuse..." the songs POV is one of disgust at the subject. This reflects the three main feelings toward this specific topic from persons involved and spectators alike.

10 - The next number in the sequence. On the right side of the words in the text of each separated section are the numbers 1-10 numbering the sections, 10 in the whole work.

5,16,8,4,2,1 - These numbers are up the left side of the text. The words and sentences have been structured around the remainder of the numbers in the sequence.

Time flew by and after only a handful of days my cell door opened and I was released, pending further investigation (PFI). I never did years of prison time. I have been arrested dozens of times for all sort of things. Never for bullshit crimes against women like domestic violence or endangering lives with drunk driving. Mostly for assaults or for possession of weapons. Doing a few days here and a few weeks there, keeping my mouth closed, retaining an attorney then being released. But I have several friends doing decades in prison. Some doing life. It would be disrespectful to act like my days in jail could compare. I only articulate it to this degree because of the importance it played in my life and the significance it had to me. It was a turning point for the way I thought about things. I feel it's important to cover the band's inception in a drug house and the fact that its first song was written in jail. Not because I'm proud but to tell the real story.

We got released to nothing. The girl I had been with for years left me because she found out about another girlfriend. One I eventually would get with who would then find out about another and so on and so forth. We had nothing to work off of so my guy brought over a garbage bag of weed on consignment so we could get back on our feet. Although we didn't know when we would be summoned to court or if anyone was still watching us.

Turned out we had been snitched on by a young cat in the neighborhood. Not a square. I don't think squares can be snitches. This was one of those types who tries to be hard, tries and act down, plays it off like he's hustlin', but the second the cops come he freaks out and gives everyone up. There had been a shootout in front of our house a few months prior. I leave a lot out incase there's reason for another book. Without getting into the details a few guys tried to kidnap myself and Gar. Shots were fired back and forth and we narrowly escaped. When police came Twerk was the only one on the scene. They arrested him for a drug warrant he had out and that's when the snitch materialized. He came from a couple blocks down to tell the police this whole story about who we were, what we were doing, how bullets were just flying everywhere, how they could've hit his house or kid etc. After a few questions and running his name he was arrested for warrants as well and put in the same car with Twerk. As they rode to the jail he continued telling the police our business. Some true some false. He didn't know we knew Twerk. No one did because we always used the back entrances of our houses which were connected. Twerk took the police car ride downtown listening to the snitch sing his songs.

All of that had to be taken care of but we also had KING. I focused on music and training. We would play our first show a few months later right in the middle unit Gar was now occupying. We destroyed the house. The plumbing was ripped out and there was water and shit everywhere. A 5 gallon bucket of white paint was thrown onto the crowd as they slipped all over each other. A room that could fit about 20 people had probably 60 packed into it. The first show let everyone know that we were completely insane.

Over the next year we would start going on little weekend show runs out of state. Doing weeklong tours to the East Coast or around the Midwest. It didn't feel like a victory at all. Instead of going to Detroit an hour away, playing for an empty room and not getting paid we were driving seven hours away to play for an empty room and not get paid. We hustled to eat and live and we had to hustle extra to cover our musical pursuit. So it goes. My thinking was that if I loved music and wanted to do it I would have to hustle way harder to live while doing what I loved which paid absolutely nothing.

9

Boogeymen

A year or two later I had a close brush with death. That day I planned on sitting at the diner reading until I was full on coffee. Later I had Muay Thai class. I had found a good school and had been training a year or so. I had the military on the back burner because of my pending cases but was optimistic I could fight them. After class I was supposed to hang out with this girl I had seen around town since my last relationship ended. I'll call her Nala because she had big ass eyes. She was the opposite of most girls I had met. She hadn't grown up the same way I did. She was a good girl. Funny how you remember everything about some days. The book I was reading was called *Learned Optimism* by psychologist Martin Seligman. I picked it up because of the subtitle, "How To Change Your Mind and Your Life." I must have read it half a dozen times. The concepts are simple and easy to understand. But a much younger version of myself, one whom needed to change his mind and his life, didn't feel that way. The book talks a lot about pessimism and optimism, self-defeat. Books like this one were small breakthroughs. Like going to jail was a small breakthrough. I hadn't completely flipped the switch in my life but I was chipping away at it over the years. I think those flipping the switch stories you hear about apply to troubles a bit more shallow. Mine ran deep and in my case I had several switches that needed flipping so it was taking some time to work on the compound problems. After finishing the book I would walk the few miles home. We were staying on the north side. My cousin had just got out of prison after a couple years and we got ourselves a place with the crew in tow. I packed my bag and walked another 5-6 miles to training. I couldn't afford the class, so to pay my fee I would clean the school and bleach the mats after each class 3-4 times a week. I did the same thing for my gym memberships.

I remember the training day was typical. For a half hour or so we ran through warm up calisthenics then rolling drills then punching drills then sparring. We'd break off into partners or groups and work on a handful of specific techniques for another hour. For the last hour or so we would open roll and work on things with a partner or our teacher.

Sometimes the coach offered me a ride home. He wouldn't drive into our neighborhood but he would drive me a couple miles closer. I would walk the rest of the way. I accepted his ride. As we drove we talked about fighting. Coach was a good fighter so I respected him. When he dropped me off I told him I'd see him next class. I shut the car door and walked into the belly of the beast, thinking nothing of it. I had made the walk my whole life. The night was quiet. My muscles ached from the training session. There was a dried sweat on my skin under my clothes. I walked in silence toward the house. This was the first time the girl would be coming over to my place. Because of my cousin who had landed a couple jobs since being released we had lights and water and was in a presentable condition. I might have to clean up a bit I felt good about it.

About ten blocks away, I entered a long desolate strip where there were no houses, no people, and no cameras. The hilly road cut right through miles of vacant lots that used to be the old GM plants. A single pair of headlights hit me in the back so I moved out of the road and onto the sidewalk. People in the hood don't use the sidewalk but we walk on the road because we're so big headed the road is a more suitable size for the giants we consider ourselves to be. A suburban pulled up alongside me and rolled the window down. There were two older cats in the front and another figure in the backseat. The older cat in the passenger seat stuck a gun out his window and pointed it at me. It looked like a 12 gauge. The old break barrel style that I imagined their grandfathers used for hunting maybe a .410. I stopped and faced the guy with the gun and the vehicle stopped with me. "Gimme the bag white boy."

I didn't care about getting shot. I didn't care about dying either. I didn't have a gun. I had taken my gun out of my bag earlier that day because I knew I would be driving home with my coach and I didn't know him like that. I must've been considerate in my younger age. I didn't even have a knife. My bag was a gym bag full of dirty clothes and boxing gloves and mitts. Nothing valuable. From an outsider perspective I had no reason not to hand it over. But since I was a gangster I grabbed my dick and said "you can get this bag." Then I stood there staring at him and waiting to be shot. A pair of headlights hit us off in the distance and the man pulled the gun back into the car and the SUV drove down the street. I turned to walk home with some relief. While I was walking I played out a bunch of possible scenarios in my head. I thought about how I would've jumped this way or grabbed the gun or did this or did that. I was really into my imagination playing through the action film scene that I thought could have taken place. After playing through countless scenarios for a few minutes I heard a single footstep directly behind me. I turned around quick, dropping my bag. There was a kid in the middle of an exaggerated wide swing. I hopped back and threw my hands out of the way out of instinct. The kid had knife in his hand and he shouted something as he swung to stab me. The knife slid through my clothes and lodged itself in my ribs. I didn't know this at the time.

A shot of adrenaline hit me. It seemed immediately I was completely aware of everything that surrounded me. I had just been in training mode the past few hours. My senses were heightened. I was aware this was the kid in the back seat. He looked young. I realized the SUV had circled the block and snuck up on me with the lights off. I knew the two men in the SUV were right behind him slowly idling by. The man with the gun had it pointed at me again. I understood all of these things instantly. The information came flooding in all at once. I recall some sort of hypersensitivity that I had never achieved in training before. Time seemed to slow. Perhaps because I understood it was training and my life wasn't on the line. A sharp pain shot around my ribs. I instinctively slammed my bicep down onto the hand that held the knife jamming it into my side more but locking his hand in and trapping it. This is what we were taught to do with kicks. To absorb the blow with the motion of the body and make the decision to trap the leg or let it go. I didn't want to let it go and give him a second chance at gutting me. I trapped the knife and slammed the palm of my hand up into the kid's nose hearing it crack. He yelled and I must have loosened up his trapped hand because the knife came out of my side cutting my bicep wide open. I didn't notice or flinch. The kid was yelling "shoot that nigga!" He couldn't shoot me though.

The drifting car was now about 20 feet away. The kid who I was now punching in the face was positioned between me and the gunman hanging out the window. The disconnect between my assailant, the gunmen and the driver was obvious. They all had different agendas. The driver drifted further away, like a getaway car anxious to leave before the bank is robbed he was crawling one or two mph similar to the way people do when they think a traffic light is about to change. The gunmen couldn't help his friend and my assailant now felt like a scared victim. I fought the kid with the knife for another few seconds which felt like minutes. I was aware of everything. The knife nicked me a couple more times, once in the arm and once in the hand as I attempted to wrestle the knife from the kid so I could return the favor of stabbing this kid into his next life. I made sure the kid stayed between me and the gun as I fought. I started to pull him as far away from the drifting car as I could. I was planning on making a break for it and running for cover. If the guy shot twice he would have to reload the gun. Maybe then I would have a chance at him. This was assuming the driver had no type of weapon.

I heard a car door shut. I understood that this was the sound of the gunmen exiting. Looking past the kid I was engaged with I saw the man moving closer toward us as the car still slowly drifted. The longer I waited to make a move the better his shot would be. When the gunman was about 12 feet away I pushed the kid toward him untangling the mess of flailing limps. This would either obstruct his view or he would instinctively catch his friend. I ran at an angle across the road toward the opposite side of the car. It was the only thing I could think of. I heard the first shot go off and tucked in to make myself a smaller target. Pieces of buckshot made ricochet sounds all around me as they hit the street and flew off in the distance. The second shot went off and pieces of buckshot hit my ankle, calf, knee and thigh. I felt like someone lit me on fire. I fell and got back up and ran toward the side of the road. I jumped down a hill into the brush in case he was reloading. I tucked myself near a bridge that passed over a river. This whole thing happened on an overpass. I watched as they jumped in the car and pulled away. I was burning all over. My arm had been cut deep. It was pouring blood and soaking through my Carhartt coat. I hadn't noticed the severity of it during the scuffle. I pulled my pant legs up to see where the pieces of buckshot went in. Perhaps this was another payment toward my karmic debt. I had a knife in my hand. I started digging out pieces of shot from my leg. Then I remember stabbing the kid. Then I thought I shouldn't dig this knife into my leg with his blood on it so I threw it into the water nearby.

I looked back and forth down the street. No one was in sight. No one had passed by during the altercation. I remember dozing off as I pressed my hand against my cut and watched the blood pour through my fingers. I don't recall feeling scared or worried. I remember feeling relieved and peaceful, slipping off into a voluntary dream state. I saw people from my past. Someone was talking to me. I didn't feel the cuts or the bullets cooking in my leg. I saw outside of linear time. I saw the past present and future running concurrently. Not like in bullshit movies but I recall having several uncontrollable thoughts all at once for I don't know how long but an understanding that seemed to hit me all at once like a dream without time. When I came to everything was clear in the world and in my head and real life was less interesting, dull, gray and more painful. I had several dreams or visions as I would prefer to call them. A dream happens and sometimes you can tell it is a series of images playing out as thoughts in your head. These things weren't thoughts contained in my head but more like the real experiences you get every minute of the day when your eyes are open. I had several formed plans and ideas and newly found beliefs and understandings. I was a different person. The experience was almost divine and I cannot articulate it in words or in writing in anyway.

When I came back to the real world I stumbled a few blocks home. While I staggered I considered the significance of the visions I just had and the people that were in them. They weren't the people I considered most important in life. Some of them I didn't even know. I was surprised at some of the people I did know that were present during this vision. I wondered if it meant anything. I wondered what the altercation looked like from an observers point of view. It's hard to judge the storm from inside the tornado. Yon and his girlfriend were the only one's home when I came through the door. I explained what had happened. I was sore and everything burned. Like I had a full body fever. My sweat was cold as I worked on peeling my clothes off. I remembered my plans to hang out with Nala. For some reason this was important enough to get in touch with her while I bled all over the house. I asked her if we could reschedule and told her I was in a small accident, I just needed a few days. Hiding things would become a habit with this one.

I climbed in the bathtub and ran the water and bled. I wasn't sure if I was dying. I didn't know if I was okay. I wasn't a doctor. I could've been bleeding til' death and I'm positive I would've sat there calmly and accepted it. That's where my head was. I thought about revenge. It became clear that getting shot was in the cards. I didn't surround myself with the best people and I didn't put myself in the safest situations. I didn't blame anyone. I take responsibility for everything that happens to me in life. I continued to bleed over the next few days. I didn't know someone could bleed for days. I thought about death a lot. I became obsessed with it. I came to terms with the idea that I wouldn't live a full life. I was at peace with being killed at any moment.

After a couple days I went to my doctor, the same one I had known since I was a kid. He looked me over and gave me a few shots. He couldn't sew anything up because I didn't come in immediately. Stitches might have trapped bacteria inside my body. He said the knife wound was deep. If it had been a bit deeper it would have found my brachial artery and emptied the blood from my body in minutes. This was a bit shocking. I told him I hallucinated some things and I had passed out. He didn't seemed to think that was unusual. He made a comment about the scars covering my arms and it made me have a think. Like a lot of kids I cut myself. Not for attention or anything as I would usually hide the hundred or more cuts all of which needed stitches none of which got them. Although as a kid I was a diagnosed dissociative and was often severely depressed I just thought it was because my life sucked and I needed to make it better. I wondered if hacking away at my skin had me fully prepared to be cut and stabbed. I didn't notice it when it happened and I was curious if I was conditioned to it. As far as the altercation I was excited by the experience. I was glad it happened and I welcomed it as part of my identity. I was cheerful in a way and grateful to be alive. Not in a new beginning second chance kind of way but quite the opposite. I wanted to make the most of what I could with my shitty life. I wanted to live fast and experience everything possible and report it in writing. Have a thousand friends and a thousand girlfriends see and feel everything I could. I didn't want to take part in the satisficing. Uninterested in a wife or children or a good job. I was inclined to remain disposable because I planned on leaving early. Meanwhile keeping my eyes open for inspiration and wisdom especially in loss and tragedy.

10

Bando Commando

After this incident we took time off from playing shows to focus on the group in accordance with the visions I had. We didn't know how long at the time only that we would stay away from the public for as long as we needed which would end up being about a year. I had a vision that would take time working out. It was just me, Gene, Twerk, and Beal. San had dropped off because his other band was picking up momentum and he couldn't be as available. That didn't matter. Me and Gene had been playing together for almost 10 years at that point. Who was going to occupy the other positions was a minor logistic at best. My head was far beyond that. Up to this point our songs were poetic. I wrote complex pieces that were very self-conscious. I wrote them this way to be competitive with other writers. Now I wanted to tell my stories in a language I thought more people could understand. Trading in the abstract prose for something more organic and representative. I wanted my 10 year old self to understand the emotions in a song were he to hear them. I became my audience of one. We had lived a life worth speaking about. It made no sense to downplay such a strength. We were disguising a defining characteristic that set us apart from the pack to fit in with a scene we clearly had nothing in common with.

We did this instinctively not deliberately but we were different. We were nothing like other groups of musicians we rubbed elbows with. They were living, we were surviving. It wasn't difficult to set ourselves apart as most of our peers considered us a dangerous gang of thugs whom which they wanted nothing to do with.

At this point we were being classified as a gang around town. We wore the same clothes, had the same tattoos, talked the same, shared beliefs, and looked out for each other. I guess we were a gang in a way that a family is a gang. I accepted the accusations because I believed we were in line with some advice Kurt Vonnegut gave in an interview to PBS. He endorsed resourcefulness and form-ing little tribes and societies of one's own, "Look, I don't mean to intimidate you, but I have a master's degree in anthropology. From the University of Chicago-- as did Saul Bellow, incidentally. But anyway, one thing I found out was that we need extended families. We need gangs. And, of course, if their tribes and clans and so forth have been dispersed by the industrial revolution by people looking for work wherever they can find it. And a nuclear family, a man, a woman and kids and a dog and cat is no survival scheme at all. Horribly vulnerable." Although there are plenty other more scientific gang or tribe endorsements across the field of sociology at this point in my life I was listening to Vonnegut. "So it goes…"

I was no longer worried about being judged for my skill as a writer. My purpose was to tell the undiluted truth. The raw stories. No one living the way we were living had a voice in heavy music. This narrative was much more common in hip hop and rap. If this meant we would be less popular so be it. That was hard to analyze anyway because it didn't exist. There wasn't much of a modern day case study. But it was my responsibility and I owed it to everyone I knew. That was my objective. Soon thereafter I wrote a song called "Brahma" that began asking *"Have you ever buried a blade in skin that wasn't your own?/Twisted and jerked the tip of the steel around the bone and sent a man home?/Tell God I'm not the boy I used to be/Oh no... I've changed... he wouldn't even recognize me."*

These were dark times. I became my toughest critic. I suffered for it but I knew I could take it. I knew it would make me stronger. The only problem with this was the people around me would have to suffer as well. I didn't care about that at the time. I felt forged in steel in a sense that no person could make a hair raise on my body for any reason. That if I chose to engage them it was with a clear head and a clear heart. I wanted to be the hardest thing to kill in the streets. My head would not be clouded with emotions and judgements like everyone else. Everything was a game that I imagined I controlled. My enemies were a joke. The police were a joke. If I was hurt or incarcerated that would mean I wasn't in control. I had struggled with this stupid kid who thought he could handle me. That wouldn't happen again. I wouldn't allow it to. Next time someone put a gun on me I'd make them eat that bitch until their lips were charred black from the charge and their teeth were laying on the next block after being blown through the back of their skull. I was the strongest opponent I had.

My wounds eventually healed. Although they ache to this day I believe they made me stronger. I believe I didn't die not because I was lucky but because I was hardened. I felt like I had been beaten down mentally over the course of my life. I stiffened to the softer aspects of the human condition. I had been let down so much I expected nothing at all. And now I was beaten down physically. When my scars healed they became calloused areas of skin where there was no feeling. I wrote *"I can't sweat through these scars and I can't feel the wind blow/ You never get used to not feeling you just know you're not like them so..."*

Eventually we would get thrown out of that house. We were focused on music and neglected supporting ourselves. We ran the bills up and were thrown out again to float around from this place to that place to sleeping in the street until we moved into a place at the beginning of summer. This particular street was called "heroin row." Its residents were junkies or dealers or the apathetic elderly couple that had lived there since before the town went to shit.

There were 9 of us in a 3 bedroom. The rest of the group was distributed around town with a girlfriend or family or piled up over capacity in another flophouse. You didn't have to be a certain kind of person to be down with us. It didn't matter if you came from a suburb outside of Flint. It didn't matter if you were 10 years younger or 10 years older. It didn't matter what you wanted to be if anything. It didn't matter what you looked like either. We looked after each other. Experiences were how our relationships were built. We were down with everybody who came along. The only thing you needed was loyalty to the crew. If you had that you were in. If you did anything disloyal you were an enemy. The psychologist Marilynn Brewer called it "optimal distinctiveness," a social psychological theory seeking to understand ingroup-outgroup differences. It asserts an individual's desire to attain an optimal balance of inclusion and distinctiveness within and between social groups and situation.

Across the street was Snoop and Gina, an OG couple from Detroit. They hustled. Shortly after we moved in we noticed they had a basketball hoop laying in their backyard. When we asked if we could throw it up in the street they said no, but over time we warmed up to one another and got the hoop out.

Next door to us was an older heavyset woman with long braids who we called "Ma" and she looked after us and us her. Her only son was an OG that had been murdered so we were like her kids.

Down the street was an elderly woman named "mamma lo ho" because she was an old school hoe. She cooked the worst food and was always making us go to the corner store and get her beer which was something we felt obligated to do because of her age.

The opposite end of the street was Dina. The blocks most reliable fiend and friend. She kept an eye on everything.

Some of us were still dirt poor teenagers and didn't care about anything. I was amongst the oldest, twenty something. We just came from being homeless so we didn't have many possessions. When we woke up we went out walking the streets finding furniture in peoples' garbage. We would carry anything from milk crates to full sofa sectionals anywhere from a block to a couple miles back to the house which was without power or water. This didn't bother us at all. In fact I remember an overall content feeling. In retrospect this was probably attributed to the hundred or so friendships we had amongst our group. We had no monetary worth but the plentiful deep as they come relationships between us made us rich in a sense.

Despite the struggle, these were happy times. We had nothing, but life was good. We were in good spirits struggling. Janis Joplin sings "freedom's just another word for nothing left to lose." We were free. We didn't have to be anywhere at any time for anyone. Freedom is something very few people prioritize. Altruism is another non-priority. These times remind me of several Emile Durkheim studies. Primarily "collective effervescence" where he expresses that "The very act of congregating is an exceptionally powerful sentiment. Once individuals are gathered together, a sort of electricity is generated from their closeness and quickly launches them to an extraordinary height of exaltation." Amongst the group "vital energies become hyper excited, the passions more intense, the sensations more powerful." As with anything scientific this was hard to comprehend at first pass but the writings by social psychologist Jonathan Haidt helped me to understand Durkheim and several other invaluable concepts.

At the beginning of the month we all got our food stamps so eating wasn't as big of a headache. We would all chip in and grill out. Our grill was a set of security bars laid across some cinder blocks on the front porch. The security bars were taken off the basement window of a neighboring house. The cinder blocks were found elsewhere and the coals were sticks found around the yard. The house had no electricity in it. This was the life.

We hung out on the porch a lot choppin' it up. Formulating ideas, talking about life, reading books and writing songs, pondering where the next meal would come from. When this grew boring we would wander into the street to shoot the basketball. When this got old we looked for girls.

Since we never left the neighborhood, one day Snoop and Gina from across the street asked us to watch their house while they were out of town. We looked up to this cat because he was older and living comfortably. We were out to prove ourselves trustworthy. When they left we remained sitting on our porch like always.

A few hours passed before some white woman came to their place knocking on the door, claiming to know Gina. She said she had left something in their house. I knew they knew her because she had been over that morning. But they said to watch the house and that's what I planned to do. It wasn't too obvious that we were watching the place and she had no reason to believe we were. The woman knocked and got no answer. I yelled across the street that they weren't home and she took off. We thought she was a fiend and paid it no mind. Fifteen minutes or so later she came back. We went inside to watch from the window. She put a chair below a window to the house and tried to climb through. We ran over and kicked the chair from under her. She fell on her stomach and the window slammed down on her. I ripped her out the window down to her shoulders. The boys were right behind me to help pull on her flailing legs. She was up higher so she ended up kicking her way in at which point we covered the exits to the house to keep her inside. She was screaming that Gina knew she was coming through. She came to the security door with the phone and a bat. She reached her hand through the door handing me the phone. Gina told me to keep her in the house until they got home that night. This earned us a little bit of trust.

After a handful of cookouts our food stamps were gone just as quick as they came. The drugs weren't happening because I had the same girl I was now trying to go legit for. I was trying to clean up my act and leave it alone mainly because she would do shit that made me feel bad like leave money in my room so I wouldn't go out and do anything illegal. I gave it an honest effort. This wasn't uncommon through the years when we had nothing we usually scraped by on the good graces of a down ass female. Someone that would give us her last and ask for nothing in return for some crazy reason. I have kept them in the dark out of respect while writing this because some are living a normal life, children, married etc. but I'm now giving them an honorable mention. Under appreciating them as always.

Without hustlin' we resorted back to a handful of tricks we used to eat. One day I remember we were hungry and only had 9 dollars. The problem was there were a dozen of us. We decided Gar and his girlfriend would go through McDonald's drive through and order four McChickens and five McDoubles. When they got to the window Warren would run by and snatch the bag. The McDonalds would replace the order and we would have eighteen burgers instead of nine. Once the woman working saw Warren coming and pulled the bag inside, trying to close the window. Warren dove into the window and ripped the bag out the woman's hands and we ran. When we weren't doing this we were calling fast food restaurants telling them they messed up a drive through order. When this didn't work we could always count on dumpster diving. At night after the pizza places closed we would climb around in their dumpsters looking for pizzas. Sometimes they would still be hot, and sometimes the police would chase us away.

We were always on some bullshit like this. Sometimes we were up and living alright. Sometimes we took a loss and that would knock us back to square one. That's just how shit went. Some days you wouldn't have a pot to piss in and other days you may have ten grand in your pocket. Either way it went as quick as it came. There was no concept of the future. I had never even thought of getting a car like a normal person may have simply because I had no ambition to leave my street or my neighborhood. Most days I wouldn't leave the porch. There was no past or future but only the now and ways to enhance the now. Also there were only a couple attainable things that would provide that enhancing excitement. These were very simple primitive things like violence, crime, girls or drugs.

This summer would be rough to say the least. When times were really tight we gravitated to our own preferred trade skills. Gar would run scams with things like credit cards and internet shit like eBay and PayPal. He was technologically capable and would often have white girls from suburban towns come through so he could take their identity. These were the types of Middle America chicks that thought they were cool for coming to the hood on the weekends and knowing a group of people like us. During the week they'd get their rocks off by telling all their square friends in school about "their crew" in "Flint town" of course omitting the fact that they had trains ran on them day in and day out. So I guess that's a kind of mutualism trading ass for clout which is found across different walks of life.

Some of us tried our hand at being a productive members of society. This was short lived. My cousin was working as a delivery driver at a pizza joint and said he could get me in. I gave it an honest effort for my relationship. This didn't last very long at all before we were collecting names, addresses and credit card numbers in a notebook so we could use later to order our own food.

After trying to force myself to make pizzas for a few weeks I quit. The money didn't match my ambitions and I couldn't stick with it. I couldn't focus on music and writing when I was in some bullshit pizza place so I just walked out the backdoor and never came back. I figured if the chick left my ass because of it I would just deal with it. I would go back to the only job I could consistently keep.

I had heard about a job opening around the neighborhood anyway. It was the lowest job you could pick up. A runner. A runner does exactly that. Runs packs of H all over town in his car or on his bike in my case. I didn't have a car and I had never ran before but I didn't care. In the morning you get a handful of packs and a phone. You count the packs back to the person who gives them to you because they always try to keep a few for themselves, deal you a short hand, say you had more than they gave you which meant you would have to pay it back later. I learned this the hard way. When the phone gets a call they tell you what they want and you tell them to meet you wherever it is you want to meet. At the end of the day you return the phone and any packs that are left over. If you run out you return to where you got the phone and get more. The guy you get the shit from is not who you work for but a kid just above your own level who doesn't really control anything. At the end of the day your incoming calls better match the amount of money you have and you get paid a little bit. This is the lowest job you can have and the most dangerous. I would try and keep this a secret from the girlfriend as long as I could. A couple weeks later she found out and made a fuss about it but stuck around.

I was riding around town one day working when I got a phone call. I knew the woman on the other end. She didn't like me. I thought it was weird she was calling. She told me Bama had been killed. I became close with him over the years. We always stayed in touch. We had different groups of friends and might go six months without seeing each other but we always picked back up where we left off. He was a mentor. This was someone I considered invincible. If there was a situation and Bam was involved Bam would be the one walking out of it when it was over. Now I was being invited to his funeral. I felt like an anchor line had been cut from around me. I pulled my bike over and sat on the curb. I didn't know what to do. You get used to losing people, you get used to death, and I was used to remaining strong. Maybe because I had to be. Maybe because everyone around me was always hysterical or irate or falling apart over something. Maybe because those around me always looked to me for strength. I remember this being one of the several months when I attended three or four funerals each month. Leaves a hole in you that no one or no thing can fill up. No one is invincible.

When Bama was killed I was lost. I didn't say much of anything because there wasn't anything to say. I gravitated toward the closest cat I knew. Snoop. Him and Gina looked out for us and we became close over the months.

Late one night I was hanging out in the street with Snoop and a few of his homeboys politickin'. A car came down the road and I recognized it as the guy that lived across the way. He was a quiet guy about mid-twenties and he kept to himself. He pulled into his driveway and we heard some kind of exchange. Apparently he pulled up and caught someone trying to climb through his window. When he pulled in they slid out and ran. He yelled after them then ran in his house to see if anything were missing.

I wasn't really paying attention and it wasn't much my business but the guy was screaming a bunch of stuff so I walked in my place to check on the girlfriend who was sleeping. Sometimes I would just look at her and wonder what the hell she was doing. She had stuck around even though I was trouble. I didn't have a house half the time and if we wanted to be alone we had to park her SUV somewhere dark and kick it in there. She would pick me up from a a new place around town every week. I was a loser. I was getting shot. I was living out of hotels. When she came over the house was loud with music and alcohol and drugs and whores until 6am rolled around and everyone passed out. This chick had an actual career. I would be sharing rooms with 2-3 other people all sleeping on the floor and she always came through and slept right there next to me. Her family friends and everyone around town including complete strangers told her I was no good. In the beginning I figured she felt sympathetic. This would change over the following years.

I walked onto the porch. The guy was still screaming in his front lawn at Snoop and his boys about how they knew someone was breaking in. This was a group of older black guys all much bigger than he was so when they slowly approached him he immediately switched his target to me, threatening me because I was younger, white and presumably less threatening to him. He was yelling and pointing making half-assed threats and walking off his porch toward me so I made sure the girl was really sleeping before figuring I would meet him halfway and ran over to him in his front lawn and punched him in the face. He backed up defensively and I continued swinging on him up his stairs to his porch and into his house. His girlfriend was screaming and calling someone on the phone. After I knocked him on the floor he curled up so I went back outside and continued hanging in the street with the guys and didn't think anything of it.

A few minutes later, a car came speeding down the road. I knew exactly what was about to happen. The guy inside had a gun and it was hanging out the window. I started walking toward the car and the man hopped out. I ducked low toward the ground moving at him as he shot once and missed. At this point I start running toward him. I had already been shot and didn't really care. I saw it as a chance to get a nice gun from him. He hopped in his car and sped off when I got to the road waving his gun out the window while driving away. Me and Snoop laughed about it a little bit then I ran inside to check on the girl who was hurled up in the corner of the room scared. The quiet man that started the incident hid in his house during the whole exchange. When I came back out Snoop and his boys were on his front lawn letting him know he would move out by tomorrow or he would be moved out.

The next morning six or eight white guys with hunting rifles, bulletproof vests and trucks pull up on the quiet man's lawn to help the couple move everything out of their house. There was some words exchanged and each party drew guns on each other and there was some screaming and yelling but no one got shot and they moved all their things out within a few hours. We never heard from them after that and their house mysteriously burned down shortly after.

If we were going to be shot at we needed protection. We knew a guy who had some guns buried in his yard and would let us hold them. These were five or six guns of all different kinds and calibers. Most were jammed up or surface rusted and hadn't been used since we didn't know when. We took them all apart and cleaned every piece. After soaking them in gasoline and wire brushing them over the course of a week we had a .22 rifle, 2 12 gauge shotguns, one pump and one hunting, a .32 handgun, a 9mm carbine and a .38 handgun. Once they were cleaned we had to make sure they worked. Anything long we would saw off so we could carry it more easily.

To test everything out we went across the cat walk to another neighborhood near a lake. We get to dumping them out and emptying them into the lake. Someone yelled "cops." I looked over and saw a cop cruiser about 50 feet away watching us with all his lights off. He had been sitting there the whole time. We took off running. He must've been doing something wrong himself because he didn't bother chasing us. We made it home on foot, now confident all of our stuff worked. If someone were to take a shot at us now we would be able to shoot back.

11

I Aint Goin Back Again

With the guns came new opportunities to get paid. Robbing. Primarily drug dealers or drug customers. We put the word out we were buying and selling when in reality we were just taking. The protocol was the same for both. If we heard you were trying to get rid of anything we acted interested in buying and met you in the middle of the day on a dead end block on the other side of ours. If you were inquiring we claimed to have whatever it was you may be after and would meet you in the same place. The block was mostly abandoned houses we tore the boards off and hung out on the porch appearing to have lived there. The mark pulled up sometimes alone in a car, sometimes with multiple people in a car. When this happened several of us would come out of the woods at strategic points surrounding the mark, forcing them to give up whatever they brought with them be it money or drugs. They always gave it up and there were no shots fired during the dozen or so scenarios. Afterward we would follow a low key trail back to our house undetected. If we got money we could pay our bills. If we got drugs we could off load them for next to nothing.

I carried a twelve gauge break barrel in my Dickies pants. This thing was sawed down to no more than 8" from one end to the other. It was called the "Pardner" because it was an H&R Pardner. It made me think of my younger days when I carried the same gun in my sweats. In hindsight over a decade had passed at this time and absolutely nothing had changed. How sad.

When the guns weren't in use we hid them in a big upright piano. We had got this piano for free off craigslist and we practiced playing regularly. The lower front board could easily be pulled off and the guns hidden inside. We would hide them whenever our square company came over or something like that. Our crib was like a shady ass after hours spot in a sense.

We didn't mess with regular people really. The kind that worked for a living and had a house and kids and things. We had problems with those who we considered were violating in some kind of way. Those who put themselves in our business. These were the targets. For example the older white guy in the new Corvette. He had no business in the neighborhood. He didn't even live in the city. He was an okay square, or so we thought. Until he turned out to be some homosexual predator. So after he tried some funny shit well my cousin had to go and set him up as well.

One day I was down by the bus station and ran into our ol' homeboy "Port". This is a dude that stays in jail more than he's free which is why he hadn't yet appeared in these stories. I chopped it up with him and gave him my number. A week or so later I was on my bike doing laundry and got a call from him saying he had a car but it was urgent. I grabbed my wet laundry and rode it home then met him on the east side. It was broad daylight and the owner of a brand new G6 SS drop top convertible parked his car in this coney island while he carpooled to work during the day. Coincidentally the same coney island I started my first job at years prior.

The back story or justification, whichever you prefer, goes as follows. Port was messing with some chick from the streets that went legitimate and had a job and a house and a life and all that. Her boyfriend owned this car and they were fighting so she put Port up on the intel. We hopped in the car and drove off like we owned it. We spent most of the day joyriding and racing around the neighborhood showing girls our new convertible. We parked it behind an abandoned house on our street when we weren't cruising around and used it as our transport for a day while we thought about what to do. We didn't have any kind of chop shop connection and we had no title to make any kind of legitimate sale so we made a genius plan to drive it to Chicago and try and sell it for 3-5k, a sure steal. Four of us drove the four hours down and parked on the south side right in the hood trying to sell this car with no title. After a full day with no luck we slept in the car and got up the next morning and continued to try again. I can understand now why no one wanted to buy a brand new car with no title for a couple grand from a couple white boys in the hood but at the time we just thought it was bad luck. We drove home after a couple days because we were out of money.

The next day we were driving through the alleys downtown. The car was full with five or six of us inside and an additional one or two in the trunk. We were going up a hill when the car shut itself off and wouldn't move. This car had OnStar and we were clueless so we thought the owner had it shut off remotely and they were tracking us on GPS. We popped the trunk and the seven of us scattered in every which way leaving the car in the alley. Five or ten minutes passed by and no one came. After 15 minutes of watching from afar we went back to the car and realized it had just ran out of gas. We put gas in it and went home.

The same day a bunch of us planned to go to the beach. We loaded up into three different cars and drove out 25 minutes to the lake. We were driving like assholes doing 120 mph, cutting people off, flicking people off you know all the things you're supposed to do when you're in a stolen car with no license etc. A few cops some miles down the expressway were sitting at the exits waiting for us to get off. They surrounded us and we laid down on the ground. The cops searched everyone and the car and hauled Port off to jail for the stolen car because he was the driver. We hopped in the other cars that were nearby watching and waiting for us to get arrested and get back home as quick as possible. Our boy would get out thereafter. Oddly enough the owner didn't want to press any charges.

We lost the car so it was back to walking around the neighborhood. At this point no one trusted us enough to do any kind of business with us and that's when things slowed up. So I just did the same thing I always did. Went to the library and dove into the books.

One night I was lying in bed with the same girl and I heard some commotion outside. I look out and some dude is in the road yelling at Snoop. His black Charger is parked on the side of the road nearby. I immediately grab the 9mm carbine. This was an all-black carbine made by HI POINT which was a company that didn't make the most reliable guns but it was best for this scenario. My girl tried talking me out of it but I ran to the back of the house where there was an easy climb onto the roof. I didn't know if there was anyone in this black Charger because the windows were tinted. I didn't want to assume there wasn't and not have a vantage point if someone came out of the car with a gun. I slowly crawled up to the peak of the roof with the carbine so I could see the whole street. I notice the guy has a pistol out and he seemed pissed. I just watched and listened. At a lull in the argument Snoop pulled out his pistol and let it hang at his side. There was a bit of a hesitation and silence so I said fuck it and stood up on the roof cocking the carbine and pulling it up to my face. They both hear this and the guy kind of backs up getting low and walking backwards toward his car staring in my direction. He left, Snoop smiled, I went back to the upset girl in bed.

This guy had just got out of jail and was coming to check Snoop for continuing to serve his customers when he got out. The next day in the middle of the day he shows back up walking down the street. Apparently they worked out a deal. I didn't understand but it was a lesson. This type of violence doesn't get anyone paid and it's always better to have friends or partners than it is enemies. Of course when violence shows up on your doorstep you do whatever you can to defend yourself but you also have to know how to read and analyze the situation instantly to make an attempt at creating an outcome that can benefit yourself. He explained how he could tell this cat could be persuaded a different way when he showed up the next day. He said at the end of the day it's just a bunch of poor people shooting each other and that doesn't get us anywhere. So I had a new perspective. Shortly after the guy in the Charger would go back to prison anyway.

One time, I got a glimpse over the fence. A whole different life-style. It came in the form of a rich, more responsible older brother figure named Tali. He was actually younger than us but he was much more mature, level-headed, hard-working, and focused. He was a friend of Warren's who showed up at the house one day out of nowhere.

Tali was a student at U of M but for some reason still had love for us. Sometimes he would take us to his house when his parents were away. The house was a castle on a lake about 30 minutes outside of Flint. He had boats and all this other shit we had no access to. When we hung out at his house we would have to move in a group because his parents had a monitoring system linked to their phones and would know Tali had people over. We would move from room to room in a pack. When someone had to shower we all went and sat in the bathroom, which is funny to remember.

I picked up a book Tali had laying around and read the first few pages. It was really good so I asked to borrow it. The book was *The Alchemist* and it opened up a lot of doors. I imagine somewhere in my subconscious the way I came to the book painted it in a certain light. I was in a multi-million dollar home. Surrounded by successful people with insight and ideas. There was furniture to sit on and carpet under my feet. It was near the lake and it was peaceful. When I took it home to read I was transported back to that environment. I felt like I had been taking the long hard road in life. On our next trip to the library we grabbed what must've been a hundred books. Whatever we could read about the business of music, books on contracts and publishing and licensing. Also finance books in general, starting with the classics from *How to Win Friends and Influence People*, *Think and Grow Rich*, *The Greatest Salesman in the World*, *The Richest Man in Babylon* and then working our way toward the more modern stuff.

Back in the neighborhood two things were happening. First we were getting evicted and had two weeks to move out of our place. Second, a police presence was developing as per usual. This could be for any number of reasons but our guess was this young girl named "Mouse" had something to do with it. She was Yon's girlfriend but they split up and she started using. She was a regular on the street and since she came along so did police. It could've been a coincidence. Snoop had moved off the street because things were getting tense. It felt like something was coming. We were too poor and too dumb to get out of the way as usual.

We were sitting inside one day and police cruisers pulled up out front. I ducked off into the piano and threw all the firearms into an acoustic guitar case, handed it to one of the twins and told him to jet. He hit the back door with it and I was right behind him with a piece of luggage of all my important things in it. Behind me everyone was scurrying to get anything out of the house for one reason or another. I hid my belongings in an abandoned shed on the block behind us. When we came back we were arrested because the nosey old people next door said they saw us hit the back fence as soon as the police pulled up. They said to show us what you ran with or they would go looking so I took them to my piece of luggage. I took them to the shed where I hid my luggage and they began searching through it while I began hoping the gun case wasn't poorly hidden in the same shed. While they searched I noticed someone had stashed a paper bag with some weed in it up in the ceiling a few feet from the officers who were now throwing my shit all over. They found nothing. They left me alone and I packed my stuff up and went back to watch them throw all of our things on the lawn.

We didn't let it get us down. We also had nowhere to go so we waited until the cops left then set our house up on the front lawn just like we had it inside. We set our living room up, our couches, bookshelves, etc., then beds off to the side all in the front yard and kept living there. It was fall and we just hoped it didn't rain. We continued on as so even continuing to invite girls over to "the house." When it got dark Snoop shined headlights on our set up so we could play cards while the car blared music. When it was time to sleep we all piled on a mattress on the curb under whatever blankets we had to keep warm because it got cold at night.

Living on the lawn we didn't have many resources so we would buy supplies to make jail cook ups with our bridge cards. Not the most desirable meal and I don't want to give up too much game but we could easily feed 8 people with a few food stamps. Crushed up hot fries and ramen, shake the seasoning in the chip bag, add hot water, roll the bag tight into a loaf shape, let it sit a while before cutting it out and adding some cheese spread and beef jerky toppings. Five bites fills you up. After a few days we started planning our next move. We couldn't stay out sleeping under a tarp for too much longer. It rained at night and we froze. On top of that it would soon be winter. The cops routinely visited the street to bother us and make sure we weren't living on the front lawn. When this happened we would just act like we were collecting our things amongst the garbage so they would leave us alone.

We had just recorded the first two songs of our new direction: "Dragging Knives" and "Brahma." We continued working on our EP, *Midwest Monsters*. During this period our name buzzed around the city and we were the single most hated group in town because of our reputation. Most knew us personally. Whether it was fighting or robbing or running a train on someone's girl. Kid shit. A lot of people around town were affected by our actions directly or indirectly. Flint isn't a big city. Word gets around and people feel the waves you create. The public opinion was people hated us because they believed we were a gang and we destroyed the local scene.

We got a lot of shows shut down and we closed a lot of venue doors for these same reasons. We were young and we were out of our minds. Our lives were hell and we brought that hell to the music and to the stage and the rest of us brought it in the crowd. It was too real and too close to home. It awoke something in people.

This would be something we would get used to in the years to come. I can't say we didn't deserve it. I'll be the first to admit we did a lot of bad things, but at the same time we did a lot of good. Most of the time this didn't matter. People gravitate toward the evil happenings around them. We definitely had a target on our backs. We were used to being believed in by no one. That didn't matter, we knew what we were going to do. If someone wasn't going to give us what we wanted we were going to take it.

We spent the following months of winter homeless. Living between the nearby McDonalds and abandoned apartments and houses. Sleeping on the street with a bag of clothes and books and a sawed off shotgun. Diving in dumpsters for food. As I write this I ask myself how someone could live the same way every day, every week, every year his whole life. Never changing. Never waking up or learning from the past. Years passed and I grew older, yet I lived the same scenarios on repeat for so long.

I was starting to know better. Looking outward existentially and judging the actions of those around me instead of listening to the bullshit they repeated day in and day out. One book at a time and one lesson at a time. Slowly morphing and changing. I was starting to think for myself and judge myself as capable of greater things. As a kid I thought I would be further when I reached this age. I had dreamed about all the places I would be. I expected more out of myself. I had failed myself. I thought I worked hard. I studied music and books and writing eight hours a day for over a decade.

I realized this was only part time. The man working a typical job routinely punched in for eight hours a day. This wasn't exceptional in any way. This kind of person seldom achieved great things. The other two thirds of the day I was fuckin' off, immersed in a lifestyle that was arguably poisonous. I wasn't coming home and kicking my feet up and drinking beer and watching TV and yelling at the kids, but I was taking part in my own version of all that either of which created no results. A change was necessary. I had to go all in. I had to take control of time. I noticed this was a big difference between those who had the things they wanted and those who just dealt with whatever life gave them. Proactivity was key.

I couldn't change the city and the way it worked. At this moment I couldn't change the violence and the economy. I could however change how I viewed all of these things and how I let these things affect me. The only thing I could change right then and there was my mind. That much was free. The slums are a misery breeding ground. Any positive choices one might pursue in life are looked down upon by adults and peers. Dreaming is shunned. Inspirational stories run rampant yet in schools we are taught as kids that so many things are impossible. Everything around me was a dream killer or an actual killer that would take your life. My family, a lot of my friends, job, school, the environment and especially myself.

Perhaps this was why I was weeding these influences out long before I could formulate this idea. Think of the studies that have shown that openness and expression go hand in hand with experiencing joy. James Pennebaker explores this in the book, *Opening Up*. A gross paraphrase of Pennebaker would be an idea that could be summed up as sick to get well. Writing about your complications and exploring them and being observant about the things that put you in your position makes it easier to understand how not to arrive in the same positions over again. This is a bit more stressful on the short term while you're immersed in it but has therapeutic long term effects. Just expressing these hard times is not enough though. The important part is to weave the memory into a coherent representation from which you derive a moral, lesson or lessons. This is a bit more helpful than the typical mantra that suggests you all too simply change your attitude toward the things in your past. It's no surprise that the lower classes shun these characteristics. Secrecy is a must for survival. Emotion is a sign of weakness. We stay locked tight and never open up and never find joy. Makes me think of a scientific study by R.M. Cooper and John Zubek who selectively bred rats who had been bred from a "maze bright" group and some from a "maze dull group." Since the maze bright and maze dull rats were reared in controlled environments the difference between the two groups could only be attributed to heredity. Cooper and Zubek placed the rats from both groups in either an empty cage with gray walls or a cage with luxuries like ramps, mirrors, swings, and tunnels. When raised in restricted environments, both groups made many errors. And when raised in the enriched environment, both made few. Since the genotypes did not change, it seems clear that the changes in behavior were caused by the changes in environment. Cooper and Zubek argued that heredity and environment always interact to produce final behavior. It bears repeating that instead of understanding these concepts people just torture clichés like "nature vs nurture" and that doesn't help anybody with anything.

I only blame one person for these shortcomings. Myself. Running the streets wasn't getting me anywhere. I had to start making changes. It wasn't going to happen overnight but something was stirring and I knew I was chasing something. Only getting shots of it here and there. I would find an answer in the work of Mihaly Csikszentmihalyi and what he describes as a state of "flow." Flow is a state in which people are so involved in an activity that nothing else seems to matter. This is a zone where you comprehend things beyond your senses and make instant decisions without processing or thinking about them. Time seems to slow down. In the case of creatives, when you fall out of flow sometimes you realize hours have passed. This isn't just high productivity. This zone can't be interrupted by getting the urge to check your phone for a social media update or hearing the neighbor's dog bark off in the distance. This is single point concentration where the only thing that exists is the task at hand. One remains intrinsically motivated and egoless.

The flow state is activated when the challenge of the task is balanced with the skill of the performer. This was the feeling I had been searching for. I had caught this autotelic experience on a lot of days spent in silence reading at the library, or walking around town writing songs, or even in the isolation of a jail cell. I had caught it training to fight and fighting. I had caught it unexpectedly the first time I was shot. I had read Ram Dass *Be Here Now* but much like Eastern wisdom it is put so simply that it is simply dismissed. I think because we as people look for a complex secret to learn as a type of cheat code. But a lot of times the answer is simple and in plain sight. Once I discovered what it was I was hell bent on achieving it at all costs. All the distractions around me were less important and I kind of started piecing things together. I worked on becoming more present

I remained close with Snoop. We drove around Flint and Detroit in his Cadillac listening to music and talking. Until he was arrested and sentenced to 15 years in prison for shooting it out with cops during a drug raid.

Mouse would get seat to federal prison after a string of robberies she committed with her junkie boyfriend. Turned out she had nothing to do with the police coming around the area after all.

Port would go back to prison for a while as well as would the rest of us here and there for stupid shit over the next few years.

I would catch a few more cases while still having the gun and drug charges hang over my head. It was a bitter pill but the US military was no longer a possibility. I had failed to remain focused on that. I would be fighting the war right here on the streets instead.

12

Life's Not Enough

Years would pass without any sign of progress. Beal would leave the band couple times and we would have to replace him with Karl. Karl was a good friend. We started playing in bands around the same time playing some of our first shows together. We recorded the *Midwest Monsters* EP and pressed a thousand copies with some money I got from my cousin who had been saving my life on a weekly basis at this point. We tried to lay it out all legitimate with a bunch of copyright logos and management companies on the packaging but in reality we had nothing. I believe it says "Management. Sneek Daddy Productions" on the case. We must have thought it sounded pretty good. Unbeknownst to us a kid from Queens who worked at Sony Publishing would get ahold of our EP. He got in touch and we talked on the phone every month or two about music and I would ask ignorant questions about the industry. We would later learn that around this time he was running around NYC screaming at every label to sign us. All of them looked at him like he was insane. We had one EP out and one video called "Murder Murder Murder." This video mainly depicted our everyday lives. It was shot over a couple days of us just hanging out. Me and my cousin shot it with a $75 digital photo camera.

This process lasted years but we didn't know much was going on and if we did we surely wouldn't have placed any stock in it. One day he called my phone and said he had met a guy at Roadrunner Records. He wanted us to hop on the phone and talk. This went on for months. We never talked about signing and I never even gave it much thought. We were never that group that was shoving anything down your throat. We surely weren't going to beg for anything. I figured if he were interested he would say something but if not I had an opportunity to learn more about the industry of music from these two guys.

One day we got a call to come to New York City and meet the people at Roadrunner. They had just been acquired by Atlantic Records. Around this time Karl wanted out of the group. He wasn't going to leave us high and dry but he didn't feel like he was in the right place as far as doing this music for a living and he knew shit was about to start movin'. To be honest neither was I. It all seemed like a bunch of fantasy land bullshit. It was what I wanted and what I had been working for but I couldn't place any faith in it. I wanted more than anything to leave the drugs and the shootings and the paranoia and the neighborhood all together. That was always the goal. But I couldn't get my hopes up for anything. I didn't know these people. We knew Beal would return to the band anyway since labels were courting us. Then we asked if he wanted to go to New York. He said it was kind of an inconvenience and we all agreed. We came up with one condition. We would entertain the idea of traveling to cities we hadn't seen before. To stay in hotels we could never afford and eat at places whose names we couldn't pronounce all on their dimes. But we would not sign a deal with anyone who didn't come to Flint to kick it with us in our neighborhood on our turf and on our own terms.

Once one major shows interest they all come knocking. We ate for free for weeks meeting a whole slew of people. We made sure to bring the whole crew out for these dinners to really get what we could out of the squares. We had recordings of two new songs that I felt were more refined and coherent. The songs were called "Fat Around The Heart" and "Desperate Lovers." One stemmed from a saying that meant "scared." It was about life on the street and how we were nothing like our peers who were scared and soft. The other was about the girl that had now finally left my ass for good. I found myself writing about her incessantly in every song. It was as if even though she were gone she was still helping me like a kind of muse. The songs resonated with everyone involved. In the end we signed with Roadrunner. They all showed up in Flint and packed into a van as we drove them around the city, showing them our neighborhood and introducing them to people. Their minds were blown when they discovered the way we lived, the conditions of our living quarters and our main acquaintances which were jack boys and prostitutes.

Anyway a record deal poured fuel on the flame. We now had a budget and more importantly the resources to pursue the projects we could only dream of before. We immediately went to work on a full length record called *Memoirs of a Murderer* but we weren't out of the woods yet. We still lived in a dope hole and all slept on the floor. When we weren't there we lived in a hotel room which was also a dope hole. The small hotel off Miller road called Hometown Inn is known for drugs and prostitution. Twelve of us lived in one hotel room piled on top of each other writing song after song. The police raided our room constantly. This is how we wrote our first record.

We had signed and were finishing up the writing process when I went and got myself into more shit. I was walking around the north one night. I walk a lot because walking through the neighborhoods is how I write songs to this day. After a few minutes of walking my mind clicks over and knows it's time to start coming up with musical passages. I guess this would be a type of walking meditation. So I was walking down the street minding my business. A car bent the block but I was caught up in what I was saying to myself. I turned down Brownell instinctively and was in the zone.

A pair of headlights behind me shut off but the sound of an engine stayed on. I started walking up in to a lawn just out of instinct. I turned around to see a handgun come out of the car window and start bustin'. I was near a telephone pole at this point so I jumped behind it and put my head against it. I felt or imagined I felt the vibrations as bullets hit the other side of the pole. I sat still for a second and the car sped off. Maybe I had a gun maybe I didn't. Maybe I shot back maybe I didn't. Nothing was said. I looked down and had been hit by a small caliber bullet and some fragments that had chipped off the pole. I hadn't even noticed. I was still standing.

I took off running toward the car immediately, a bit high on adrenaline. It sped away around the corner and out of sight. I didn't stop running for a few miles down the road. I grabbed my phone to call Warren. He had a car. I told him where I was and hid off the road in some bushes. I felt a throbbing in my hip now. I pulled my pants down and could feel where pieces of bullets were buried in the side of my hip. I couldn't see the wounds too clearly. Headlights turned down the street and my friend stopped in the road. I hopped in his car. This dude stopped to get gas on the way home while I bled in his vehicle. He took me back to the dope house in which we're writing the album and we decided we needed to dig these fragments out. Three or four fragments were visible. I sat on the toilet and Warren started digging into the holes with the file on a pair of nail clippers and some tweezers. This was the painful part. I kicked against the wall ripping the toilet out of the floor causing water to spray everywhere as I bled all over the bathroom and my friend dug into my skin. This was a real sight to see. Almost funny. We got most of the pieces out which is how we knew it was a small caliber. I kept the spent bullets as a souvenir.

I kept this a secret from the label. I had heard labels usually shy away from this kind of thing. They don't want their investment to be any riskier than it already is. I had a refreshed outlook writing the rest of the record.

When we went to record our record we didn't go to a big studio in the city. We went to a friend's house. A Canadian Juggalo named Josh Schroeder in his home studio 40 minutes north of Flint. The place we recorded our last demos. We had a real chemistry with this character.

The record was passed around behind the scenes and people began whispering about it. So much so that Metal Hammer wanted to fly over from the UK to see it for themselves. They followed us around the city for a day and dubbed us "the most dangerous group in music." I guess in a way they were right. We were dangerous in a way that if you fucked with one of us you would have to kill us all to stop us from getting after you. But we weren't dangerous to the point where we were going to get up on stage and shoot somebody to get the approval of a bunch of middle American white suburban squares. Shedding a light on the city was part of our mission. We felt it was necessary to understand the origin of the band. On top of this we also thought raising awareness might prompt some kind of change be it from within or from the outside. Okay maybe that was a bit of revisionist history optimism.

We released an EP called *proem* which was exactly that. A precursor to the record that was coming. We released a video for the song "Killem All" which was the world's first look at the band. This video didn't feature us much. We didn't care about fame or recognition. It showed viewers around Flint and introduced them to its people. A large part of the video is also comprised of surveillance footage, crime videos and news clippings of violence that was happening around the world. When the crew does appear we are disguised with a facemark bandana I had sketched out and had printed. We knew the police would see us and we didn't want to give them any kind of insight they didn't earn. A lot of us couldn't be around each other. A lot of us couldn't be around guns. Half of our crew was wanted for felony offenses or had outstanding warrants. The other half were on house arrest or probation. We had to obscure things a bit. Of course it didn't help that people started robbing convenience stores in the same bandanas.

The goal of the video was to show that violence was a worldwide epidemic. We wanted to hold up the mirror in a way that struck a nerve in everyone. Sympathizing with those struggling and waking up those who aren't well aware of this reality. Instead, the piece was seen as controversial and offensive and made a lot of people upset. Which is an obvious telling sign. The media ate it up.

Our next move was to hit the Rock on the Range music festival, a Midwest radio rock festival with an attendance of around 100,000 people. With only our video and EP buzzing around we could finally show everyone the face of the animal. There were 10 of us onstage in masks with AK 47's for the show. In my opinion live it looked like a rock n roll Wu Tang Clan so we achieved that goal. The media wrote more crazy stuff about us that we would never read. But people in the Midwest were all too familiar with us. They loved what they saw. There was finally a group telling their stories. We stood for the people.

Soon after, we were asked to play Download Festival. A British rock festival with an attendance over 100,000 people. Download is legendary. But we would have to fly to London. Our team didn't even know if this was a possibility given our criminal records. They went to work. A lot of us couldn't be cleared so we focused on the members of the bands that we thought had a chance of being allowed in another country. Once we were told it was possible, we confirmed.

On the ride to the airport we couldn't believe we were about to leave the country. We had never been anywhere. We couldn't even visualize what the rest of the world might be like. But we were ready to show everyone across Europe what exactly Flint, Michigan was all about. Or so we thought. Upon arrival at the airport we were surrounded by the Michigan State Police task force. They arrested me and Gene on the spot. We had no idea why as we sat there in cuffs. It could have been for any number of things. I assumed it was from the week prior where we were in a shootout at a basketball court. I didn't know if anyone from the other side had been hit or died but I did know police had been looking around town for a 20 something year old white male with red hair.

After awhile the police claimed it was for some kind of "assault w/ intent" but this didn't clarify much of anything either. We were mainly worried that someone had died. We were photographed in cuffs on the platform and when the press got ahold of it they went wild. We were the most talked about group on the rock n roll scene.

I would reach out on the phone to a homeboy Zack. We had respect for each other and kicked over the years. Me, Zack, Gene and Sid had never been into drugs or alcohol which was another common bond. He was into hardcore music which I didn't know shit about but he had recently moved out of state and escaped Flint which I thought was crazy since he had the city tattooed on his face. I also thought it was commendable. Anyway he got to tellin' me the world wrote us off. They said we fucked up our chance and that was it. They really thought we were done for after just a couple months. But we weren't fazed at all. Jail wasn't going to stop us. Nothing was. The only way we could be stopped was death. Jail was just a minor setback. When we got into the bullpen downtown, we were embraced and celebrated. We were amongst friends and family and everyone was getting wild. They knew we were supposed to be in Europe playing yet we were sitting in there with them. They carved the words to our songs in the walls of their cells, they screamed at CO's to let us out so we could go to Europe and represent. This wasn't a failure. This was who we were. While the internet was claiming we were fucked we were experiencing one of the best times we could remember. Me and Gene couldn't stop smiling. We were amongst the people. I wrote a verse about it as usual.

"Came out talkin about crime they said that I was fakin
Then I went to jail I wasn't fake but they kept hatin
I put a microscope on a city they didn't care about
Why was I surprised when critics didn't care for what I put out?
So this ain't for the editors
This is for the predators
The 50 some odd men in the bullpen
Arrested at the airport supposed to be in London
They said we fucked it up and that our careers were done then
Meanwhile I'm embraced by the worlds waste
We share the same tattoos all in the database
They carve my words on the walls in their cells
They said "It doesn't take the pain away but it helps"
So this ain't for your column
I solemnly swore to my city and its people that I got em
I'm more comfortable in the cage than on the stage
What the fuck would you do if you were in my place?
Would you just ignore them and not mention the place?
And turn your back on them and let the world forget their names
When all they ever wanted was for you to achieve fame
And tell their story for them cuz they knew they would be slain

Sad part about it is I told someone else to tell mine
Cuz growin up as a kid all I pictured was my dyin
And how I've made it this far you gotta believe in luck
Cuz how I'm livin lately its like I don't give a fuck
And Ive been shot up and stabbed up and thrown into the cell
And I beat all the odds that said I wouldn't live to tell
And now I'm tellin the whole world what life is like in hell
And I haven't made it out I'm still knee deep in gunshells
And casings and cases I caught cuz I wouldn't tell
Industry looks at me like I'm a hard sell
And often I wanna kill myself I don't know why I'm waitin
Things I'm supposed to love and care about I feel are quickly fading
But its only me that's changing, no one can take a thing from me
And I've taken human lives and Ive used it to make money
So next time you say you're a monster you better think twice
Cuz you can take your masks off I wear these scars for life
And if I come off like a man know that I'm just playing nice
And if I come off like I understand know were nothing alike
I was the man you are now as a kid
And the thing I am right now I can't explain what it is
But if you were me and they were shootin for your head
And you kept a loaded gun to prevent your own death
And you lived on the run wanted by the law
Cuz crimes you committed to survive were never ever solved
And when you closed your eyes you saw kids being killed
It's not fantasies its memories of kids being killed
What would you write about in your songs?
When all you see is dead friends and get prison calls all day long
These motherfuckers want the knife blade in their rib cage
If they catch me on the wrong day

Meet me middle of the night in the cold and ice
And neither of us leave unless it's with the others life"

We would eventually find out it wasn't too serious. It wasn't about the most recent shootout so I guess I'll leave those details for the next volume. We got lucky once again. Some kid we had been in a fight with was put into a coma and they were just now coming after us a year later. It wasn't a civil infraction but it could've been much worse. After a couple days we were bonded out so we could fight the case. When we left, we told everyone we wouldn't let them down. Afterward we left with a purpose we didn't know we had beforehand.

My phone was ringing off the hook and everyone wanted answers. But I had made a promise to my bunkie so before I talked to anyone I had something to do. When we learned I was getting out he gave me a phone number and a detailed description of where he had hid some money. I committed it to memory. I called the number and there was a girl on the other end. My bunkie's girlfriend. I explained who I was and walked her through the house I had never been in to find his stash so she could come bail him out. She was ecstatic and screaming into the phone. I haven't seen him since but I hope he is well.

We began a handful of court hearings. Then to rehearsal. Then to a court hearing. Then back to rehearsal. During this time we were given the opportunity to open up the Rockstar Mayhem Festival. A heavy music summer festival tour that picked up where Ozzfest left off. We were anxious to get out on the road and begin working on the things we had dreamed of doing. It was as if our past lives were creeping up on us. We had to keep moving. It was on our heels. Reminds me of the old Robert Johnson song, "Hellhound on my Trail."

If it was a US tour all 15 of us were going. We got on a bus and headed out on the road. There weren't enough beds but we were used to sharing a small space. We had just moved out of a hotel room and the bus was far nicer than most of our houses. Gene and I had to stay behind for a court hearing. We sent a bus with Twerk, Beal and crew in tow. These were the same characters that had always been around. Kat was there. Sneek was there. One half the twins was there. Warren was there. Flynn who was living in his truck 10 years prior was now getting off house arrest. He had just had his tether cut off and was running for the bus as it was leaving town. Warren who was diving through McDonalds windows years prior was aboard amongst everyone else. We had no clue what we were doing as the bus pulled out of town.

Gene and I went to get clothes for court the next day. The plan was to send the guys to the West Coast which was a couple days drive. We would go to court and ask for more time on the case due to the tour. We had attorney Mike Manley who is known around Flint and we felt good about our odds. If we were granted more time we would fly to LA to meet up with the guys at a rehearsal space where the tour would start. If we weren't, we would have to fight the case flying back and forth the duration of the tour.

The next day the courtroom was full. Every bench. Blacks, whites and Hispanics all in black. No witnesses would testify against me. The victim was unclear about who was who. Manley worked his magic and I was off the hook. That was our main objective since I had a criminal past and we had overseas offers on the table. If necessary Gene would shoulder all the blame. For this reason he wasn't off the hook yet. He was scheduled to return to court the following month and would have to fly back and forth while we were on the tour. None of this bothered us. We were used to the odds being rigged. We left court and got on a plane to LA. We had made it. Pending court cases, absconding from probation, wanted men on the run we embarked on the US to show everyone what people had been talking about. We had just released our music video for "Fat Around the Heart" which we filmed in the neighborhoods we grew up in with all of our friends. We were out for blood. To fuck this whole music thing over.

A few months on the road was weird. I don't know how to describe it but I tried minding my own business and reading my books and just hangin' with the boys. We got to see a bunch of shit we thought we'd never see together. Back home they wanted to imprison us but when the 15 of us walked on stage thousands of people lost their minds.

When we got back from our first tour we weren't hard to find. That's when the lifestyle caught up with us yet again. It was as if the city caught fire when we pulled away on that tour bus and what we came home to was a hell where everyone was out for themselves. We started getting arrested one by one. We couldn't outrun our past. Although we were retired from all those things and doing our best to focus on music and be positive and productive. There were consequences and pounds of flesh to give out. It was only fair. When we came home from the tour we were still in court for Gene's case. Amongst this it was one situation after another. Things had definitely changed. That's when I realized there were flaws in a lot of the things I thought were concrete. Like loyalty. It is preached and praised everywhere in the street but they never give you a disclaimer. There is such thing as being too loyal. When you are too loyal to others you can be misused by them without any effort at all. Being loyal to someone who isn't as loyal to you or to themselves allows you to be exploited. This is something you have to be able to read and avoid because in the end the loyal man hangs while the snakes move onward and continue to play the game. Blind loyalty can allow others to misuse you.

Meanwhile the UK and Europe were clamoring to see us. I didn't even know they were two different places but we thought it was important to get over there and make up for missing Download festival just a couple months before. We went to the airport and joked with TSA about how they had just seen us get hauled off a couple months before. We did a couple weeks overseas. We hit the UK and a little bit of Germany. It was a wake-up call that maybe we weren't so different. Seeing proof that music was a universal language. We saw places we had only heard about. People living on the other side of the world whom we thought we had nothing in common with had been moved by our message. They packed rooms and sang every word. People had KING tattoos all over them like our people at home. It felt as if I were in the crowd watching the show.

When we came home it was back in the courtroom to finish off Gene's case. He was eventually acquitted as well. A few weeks later, we were asked to go on a world tour opening up for Korn and

Slipknot. The tour would start in October of 2014 in California with the annual Knotfest. We pulled no punches on this show. We smashed every piece of gear we could grab. I climbed the truss and we fought each other on stage. We lost it. It sounded like shit but we didn't care. This continued through December, hitting all major US cities and taking a couple weeks off for Christmas. Korn continued to play shows when the tour took a holiday break so we stayed on with them playing to their welcoming fans.

In January the tour was back on overseas to the UK, Europe, Ireland, Luxembourg, Hungary and Finland, amongst a bunch of others. On the Slipknot and Korn tour we just tried to stay out of everyone's way. The rooms were huge. We had never played arenas before. Some places like Birmingham England had 15,000 people packed in them. This was a whole different ball game. Of course we didn't let anyone see us sweat. We believed we belonged there so we acted like we belonged there but in my head I went back and forth one day feeling severe imposter syndrome the next feeling survivors guilt. During this tour I missed 6 funerals over the span of 10 days. On top of that my dogs Black and E were just arrested for gun possession, armed robbery and attempted murder. I knew what I should be doing but it wasn't what I wanted to be doing.

At the same time were on the road with legends. Two groups we had been studying for years. I didn't want to miss an opportunity. We knew every song they had written and every event in there career. When we sat and talked with them we tried to act like we were learning for the first time. It was an honor to play with these guys on that tour. We watched their shows every night no matter what. We learned an enormous amount. They made us hold ourselves to a much higher standard. We're indebted to both groups and were proud to have gained them as friends and mentors. The tour ended in February. At that point our record had been out for six months. To say we hit the ground running would be an understatement.

We were home a couple weeks in February before it was time to fly to Australia for Soundwave Festival. An annual festival that hits Melbourne, Brisbane, Adelaide and Sydney. We were back with Slipknot and playing with other groups we grew up on and respected like Marilyn Manson and the Smashing Pumpkins. We shared a hotel with our friends from The Swellers. They came up the same time we did playing that same small venue we practiced in all those years. We had known each other since we were kids. It was kind of funny to travel halfway across the world and play with your friends from back home for the first time in 15 years.

Australia, like most of the places we had been, blew our minds. I think mostly because of how far away it is. I'm sure no one from my block has been to this place. It was a long trip but when we got on the stage there were rows of kids with KING bandanas covering their faces even in the 100 degree weather. We couldn't believe what we were doing had made it this far. Every once in a while I would do an interview or talk to somebody and I had no clue what to say or how to say it. Aside from not knowing how to answer questions I didn't see myself as the same human species as anyone around me. All I could think about was the boys back home. I couldn't put my mind together to answer the simplest of questions. It remains like that today. I simply don't know what to say or how I'm supposed to act. They do have books written on how a bottom feeding loser can effectively appear as a hero or role model to the rest of the world but executing is different animal I guess.

Sometimes when we were playing the guys will be waiting for me to cue a song or say some words etc. Between songs as a stood there on stage I would stare out into the distance. The crowd would stare at me expecting something like they do from all frontmen. All my boys would sit silently I imagine thinking the same thing I was thinking. As I stood in front of thousands of people in a country I could barely pronounce. I thought of my city. I thought of my neighborhood. I remembered earlier that same year I had been laying in someone's bushes. I had bullets flying all around me. I thought of those days we spent living on our front lawn. I looked at the scars all over myself. I thought of a kid I met in jail that carved my lyrics into his arm with a razor. I thought of a party we recently had. I thought of the girls dancing and the guys laughing as they drank and smoked. Sid was home from the Middle East. I thought of the unbreakable bonds we had built. The most important thing that was happening to them back at home was me standing right here. I thought of my brothers and sisters. Wondered what my mom was doing. Wondered if my dad was still kickin'. I thought of the friends I had buried. I wondered if they had died for me to be here. I thought of their children. I thought of my girl that had left after all those years. I wished she could have met me then when I was a "normal person." When I was acceptable and had "achieved something." When I was somebody. A strong desire came over me. One I had felt several times over the years. A desire I understood and knew well. The desire to kill myself.

13

Wade In The Water

By the time we got back from Australia in March, members of the crew were dropping like flies. Jail. Drugs. Falling off. Prison. Betrayal. Death. We were dwindling as a group. Our city had been changing as well. It was like it was being split down the middle. An emergency manager had been appointed to Flint after the city declared it was in the midst of a financial emergency. The city had a large deficit and started securing emergency loans. Private companies went to work gentrifying areas starting around the colleges and universities.

Along with these changes Flint received a chunk of funding. That's when the Michigan State Police came. These boys get paid twice as much as our own police to patrol streets they know nothing about to work with people they don't understand. The jails filled quickly. Though things seemed like they were looking up at least for the economy and the overall city, those living on the outside saw a different picture.

There was a genius plan to raise deposits on anything they could to draw funding. Renters who would have to pay a $100 water deposit before no had to come up with $350-400 to get their water turned on. When the water deposit became more than a month's rent it pushed a lot of low income renters out of the city of Flint where prices were more typical. On top of this there was a plan circulating to switch the water supply.

We had drawn water since the 60's from Detroit, who got it from Lake Huron. Now officials planned to make the switch to save money. Their source would be the Flint River. Anyone familiar with the river knows its reputation. A lot of us thought this was a joke. The auto industry had been filling it with toxins for decades. It had been contaminated since anyone could remember. It had been tested over the years and found to be corrosive with an endless list of toxins, fecal coliform bacteria, oil, and plant nutrients, among other things.

This water supply was switched anyway. They just told us all to boil our water before using it. Meanwhile they were running live military drills throughout our neighborhoods. Military exercises authorized by the Pentagon were taking place around the clock throughout the city. Live fire drills complete with bombs and RPG's ran around the clock, I guess they figured we were used to it.

Shortly after, what was left of GM started complaining that the water they were using in their machines primarily to paint the cars was damaging them. The government hopped in and gave them a special hook-up to Lake Huron that cost almost a half a million dollars while leaving the city to drink and bathe in water GM refused to spray cars with. The Kat was hospitalized with lead poisoning after he disregarded the news and continued drinking the water.

People boiling the water were soon advised not to when everyone realized lead cannot be boiled out and as the people in our city became sick this thing called music kept tugging at our hoodies.

We were dropped in the middle of this during the few weeks we were home before hitting the road with one of the biggest independent rappers in the world TECH N9NE on a 48 show rap tour across the US spanning from April to June. The bill was a challenge. We had just been on a long arena tour and had to transition back to smaller places. On top of this it was a rap bill. We sat in the middle of a bill full of trap rap, back pack rap and hip hop etc. It was a challenge we embraced. Not a typical move for a heavy band to make but it made perfect sense to us being fans of Tech. Once we arrived on the tour we realized it wasn't as big a challenge as we imagined. The tour was the most comfortable we had been on. We were surrounded by people just like us for the first time since we started playing music.

We left on the road while working on a mixtape we would drop while on the tour. We collaborated with rappers like Zuse, Trick Trick, Freddie Gibbs and our homeboys from the neighborhood GameSpittaz. We linked up with DJ Drama and *Midwest Monsters 2* was officially a "Gangsta Grillz" production. This was another first in heavy music. The cover of the mixtape was a photograph of us just before we debuted to the world as a group. This is how we looked when this thing came out to the world. Now most of the people in the photo weren't around anymore. This was a frozen moment in time and I hate looking at the photo. It's painful.

The mixtape confused a lot of people. As with most things we do, critics thought it was shit. We thought it was a creative milestone for us. We saw it as a boundary pusher blending rap and heavy music together in an organic fashion, unlike the rap metal movement that had happened years before. We wanted this to expand music consciousness. We were interested in aligning ourselves with like-minded individuals and artists who shared a similar struggle. We seldom found this in our own genre but it never occurred to us to look only within our genre. We hadn't been raised that way.

A song on the tape called "Let Me Be Alone" starts by saying *"I feel like I shouldn't talk about the knives or the guns when they can't even serve water in the schools where I'm from."* This touches on the crisis happening at home. They were calling for drinking fountains in schools to be taped off and bottled water was starting to be trucked into schools. We felt it was our duty to address the issue because it seemed to be falling on deaf ears.

Shortly after we got home from the Tech tour, water was the only thing anyone wanted to talk about. It was all over our news and it was everywhere we looked. It could no longer be ignored or swept under the rug. The president declared a state of emergency for the city and it became worldwide news. Cameras were everywhere and our neighborhoods and people were all over the television. Celebrities, foundations, companies, and individuals were sending cases of water. The National Guard was sent to help distribute water around the clock at the fire stations all over town. We dove in and started doing what we could donating water to these stations or leaving them piled up on street corners throughout our neighborhoods for those who could not drive to the fire stations to pick up and haul cases in their cars. This was a temporary fix while the government figured out how they would procure the billions of dollars it would cost to swap out a great deal of the sewer system that was pumping water with over 900 times the safe amount of lead into homes now for years. It has been estimated it will take 15 years to remedy. The housing market plummeted. The President and the Governor did stupid shit like go on TV and drink glasses of water like that means anything. Meanwhile the first person to file a lawsuit against the city about the water was found shot dead. On top of this an executive office in Flint's City Hall where water files were kept was "burglarized" and documents pertaining to the incident came up missing and another couple people came up dead. Nowadays people mention it as if the problem has been remedied at all. I think this is because CNN has moved on to the next hot button topic but the truth is it hasn't. Instead and I think this is because the attention is now off us as a city they have reinstated the water bills charging more than ever for the poisonous shit.

This is the place we were born. This is the environment we were conceived in. This is the kind of life we live. This is why we look and sound the way we do. This is why we're interested in shedding light on the underbelly and exposing the problems rather than cheering about a few positive strides. We're interested in treating the cause not the symptoms. I hope Flint turns around completely. I hope I'm still around to see it.

Most of all, I hope we can turn it around for ourselves as a people. This is where my loyalty lies. With the people. Like the ones who whooped my ass at the basketball court as a kid, like the ones I recorded songs into an answering machine with, like the ones who made a swimming pool in the bed of the truck, like 100 of us packed into our house when the music is loud and the girls are dancing and the guys are yelling shit, like the ones in the over-crowded bull pens and jails, the dirt poor, the ones struggling without a pot to piss in, the ones putting plastic on the bicycle seat to ride in the rain, or waiting at the bus stop with their dirty laundry, or still sharing bath water, the ones without anywhere to be or anyone to answer to. With the people.

I love y'all.

Epilogue

I'm proud to be from Flint, MI. I'm proud to have grown up in a city facing constant adversity. As anyone who has struggled will tell you, they know that without it they wouldn't be who they are. Being born and raised in troubled times, earning everything we received – that can never be taken away from us. If my city is one day gentrified and does a complete 180 it won't matter at all. It'll never change the decades we spent struggling. We will always have that.

No matter how things change it'll always be a part of who we are. People on the outside don't understand this. If you spend 30 years struggling it doesn't go away over night. It doesn't go away ever. Nothing changes after a year or two or five or ten. You still see the angles in every place you walk into, you still read everyone like a potential threat or enemy, you're still quick to react, you still check the car before you get in, or the mirror in case someone's following you. You never leave your gun at the house, you always have an out and you never fully trust the next guy because everyone always wants something. It's embedded in your psyche. It's instinctive.

To put yourself in the same shoes you would have to have fought to survive on a daily basis for years. It's what I was built for. It's what

I can handle. It's easy to think of yourself as good person when you've never been tried. When you've never struggled or starved. When you have a roof over your head and your warm and you're fed and you know you're safe when you lay down at night and you know where you'll be tomorrow and next week. When you have no reason to physically compete with another man.

So whoever you are reading this, never stop working through the struggle. Don't create a back-up plan. Observe as much as you can. Don't talk so much. Cross the bridge and burn it behind you. Give yourself no choice. Define the things you want and run toward them. When everyone works, work. When everyone stops working, work. When everyone goes to sleep, work. When you achieve what you think you were working for, work even more because there are things beyond your goals you may not have been able to previously conceive. Have tunnel vision. Leave it all on the page. Lose anyone who isn't helping you get to where you're going even if that means everyone. Friends, brothers, sisters, parents, partners. If they aren't helping you they are hurting you. Fuck em.

Flint Michigan rules the world.